ADVANCES IN ECONOMETRICS - THEORY AND APPLICATIONS

Edited by **Miroslav Verbič**

Advances in Econometrics - Theory and Applications
Edited by Miroslav Verbič

Published by InTech
Janeza Trdine 9, 51000 Rijeka, Croatia

Publishing Process Manager Iva Lipovic

Technical Editor Teodora Smiljanic

Cover Designer InTech Design Team

Additional hard copies can be obtained from orders@intechopen.com

Advances in Econometrics - Theory and Applications, Edited by Miroslav Verbič
p. cm.
ISBN 978-953-307-503-7

For EU product safety concerns:
IN TECH d.o.o., Prolaz Marije Krucifikse Kozulić 3, 51000 Rijeka, Croatia,
info@intechopen.com or visit our website at intechopen.com.

Meet the editor

Dr. Miroslav Verbič is an assistant professor of econometrics and an assistant professor of finance at the University of Ljubljana, and a senior research fellow at the Institute for Economic Research in Ljubljana. His research interests include econometric modelling, general equilibrium modelling, asset pricing modelling, social security analysis, welfare economics, and environmental economics. He teaches econometrics at the graduate and undergraduate level at the University of Ljubljana, and abroad as a visiting professor. He is the author of two scientific monographs and more than twenty-five scientific articles, indexed in international publications. He is promoting his research activity as a member of Econometric Society, IARIW, and other professional associations. He is also engaged in several projects commissioned by the Slovenian government and the EU Commission.

Contents

Preface

Econometrics is a (sub)discipline of economics concerned with the development of economic science in line with mathematics and statistics. Theoretical econometrics studies statistical properties of econometric procedures; applied econometrics includes the application of econometric methods to assess economic theories and the development and use of econometric models. The term "econometrics" first appeared one century ago, while the discipline really got the momentum in the 1930s with the founding of Econometric Society. Nowadays, econometrics is becoming a highly developed and highly mathematicized array of its own (sub)disciplines. And it should be this way, as economies are becoming increasingly complex, and scientific economic analyses require progressively thorough knowledge of solid quantitative methods. This was especially obvious during the recent global financial and economic crisis. As my graduate professor of econometrics, Dr. Jan F. Kiviet used to say: "Economics deserves hard methods." This book thus provides a recent insight on some key issues in econometric theory and applications.

The first three chapters focus on recent advances in econometric theory. The first chapter explores non-parametric (NP) estimation with a priori assumptions on neither the functional relations nor on the observed data. This appears to be the most general possible form on the purpose of econometrics; finding the functional form that underlies the data without making a priori restrictions or assumptions that can bias the search. In seeking the boundaries of the possible, one runs against a sharp dividing line that defines a necessary and sufficient condition for successful NP estimation. This condition is denominated "The limits of econometrics", and it is found somewhat surprisingly that it is equal to the classic statistical assumption on the relative likelihood of bounded and unbounded events.

The second chapter considers the traditional approach to the persistence properties of time series, i.e. the unit root testing and the median-unbiasedness method. The latter is used to estimate e.g. the AR(1) coefficients to investigate the persistence behaviour, due to the near unit root bias and resulting lack of distribution. Here it is shown that in order to calculate half-life from an AR(1) model, the instrument generating function (IGF) estimator is not only an asymptotically normal estimator, but also an easy-to-use alternative to the median-unbiasedness approach. An unrestricted FM-AR(p) model is proposed, a slight extension of the FM-VAR method, to estimate coefficients directly.

The third chapter proposes various classes of seasonal volatility models. Time series processes are considered, such as AR and RCA processes, with multiplicative seasonal GARCH errors and SV errors. The multiplicative seasonal volatility models are suitable for time series where autocorrelation exists at seasonal and at adjacent non-seasonal lags. The models introduced here extend and complement the existing volatility models in the literature to seasonal volatility models by introducing more general structures.

The last three chapters are dedicated to recent econometric applications. The fourth chapter focuses on the impacts of government-sponsored training programs aimed at disadvantaged male youths on their labour market transitions. A continuous time duration model is applied to estimate the density of duration times, controlling for the endogeneity of an individual's training status. The sensitivity of parameter estimates is investigated by comparing a typical non-parametric specification and a series of parametric two-factor loading models. These models implicitly assume that the intensity of transitions is related to the state of destination. Additionally, a parametric three-factor loading model is estimated. The novelty of this specification lies in the fact that the intensities of transitions are related to both the state of destination and the state of origin.

The fifth chapter extends the existing research on the returns to human capital accumulation that differentiates between the self-employed and wage earners. This is carried out by providing evidence in a cross-country framework using a homogenous database, which mitigates the problems associated with the existence of different data sources across countries, by using a panel data approach that is useful in dealing with endogeneity and selectivity biases, as well as unobserved heterogeneity, and by applying an efficient estimation method that allows for the correlation between individual effects and time-invariant regressors, and that avoids the insecurity associated with the choice of the appropriate instruments.

The last chapter investigates the international demand for tourism in two neighbouring Scandinavian regions by specifying separate equations that include the relevant information. A period of transition is analyzed from lower levels of integration to more intense integration, globalization, competitiveness, and high levels of income and welfare. Instead of being estimated equation-by-equation using standard ordinary least squares, which is a consistent estimation method, the equations are estimated using the generally more efficient iterative seemingly unrelated regression (ISUR) approach, which amounts to feasible generalized least squares with a specific form of the variance-covariance matrix.

The book contains up-to-date publications of leading experts. The references at the end of each chapter provide a starting point to acquire a deeper knowledge on the state of the art. The edition is intended to furnish valuable recent information to the professionals involved in developing econometric theory and performing econometric applications.

Lastly, I would like to thank all the authors for their excellent contributions in different areas covered by this book, and the InTech team, especially the process manager Ms. Iva Lipović, for their support and patience during the whole process of creating this book. I dedicate this book to my mother Ana Verbič and my recently deceased father Miroslav Verbič.

Miroslav Verbič
University of Ljubljana,
Slovenia

Part 1

Recent Advances in Econometric Theory

1

The Limits of Mathematics and NP Estimation in Hilbert Spaces

Graciela Chichilnisky*
Columbia University, New York
USA

1. Introduction

Non-Parametric (NP) estimation seeks the most general way to find a functional form that fits observed data. Any parametric assumption places a somewhat unnatural *apriori* restriction on the problem. For example linear estimation assumes from the outset that the functional forms described by the data are linear. This is a strong assumption that is often incorrect and prevents us from seeing the essential non-linear nature of economics. Indeed market clearing conditions are typically non-linear and therefore market behavior is not properly described by linear equations. Parametric estimation is therefore a "straight-jacket" that limits or distorts our perception of the world.

But how general is the *NP* philosophy? How far does it go? Are there limits to *NP* econometric estimation, can we assume nothing at all about the parameters of the problem and still obtain successful statistical tests that disclose the funcional forms behind the observed data? This chapter explores the limits to our ability to extend *NP* estimation. Considering the success of *NP* estimation in bounded or compact domains, the chapter seeks ways to identify the limits of extending it from bounded intervals to the entire real line R^+, so as to avoid artificial constraints that contradict the intention of NP estimation. The bounded sample approach is not new. In 1985 Rex Bergstrom (1985) constructed a non - parametric *(NP)* estimator for non-linear models with bounded sample spaces, using techniques of Hilbert spaces[1] a type of space I introduced in Economics (Chichilnisky, 1977). His article is simple, elegant and general, but requires an *a priori* bound on observed data that conflicts with the spirit of *NP* estimation. This chapter extends these original results to *unbounded* sample spaces such as the positive real line R^+,[2] using earlier work (Chichilnisky 1976, 1977, 1996, 2000, 2006, 2009, 2010a, 2010b and 2011). We find a sharp dividing line, a condition that is both necessary and sufficient for extending *NP* estimation from bounded intervals to the entire real line. The clue

---

*UNESCO Professor of Mathematics and Economics, and Director, Columbia Consortium for Risk Management, Columbia University, New York. This chapter was based on an invited address at a conference at the University of Essex in May 2006, honoring Rex Bergstrom's memory. I thank the participants for valuable comments and particularly Peter Phillips, the organizer. I am also grateful to William Barnett of the University of Kansas, the participants of a Statistics Department seminar at Columbia University, the Econometrics Seminar at the Economics Department of Columbia University, and particularly Victor De La Pena, Chris Heyde, Marc Henry and Dennis Kristensen, for helpful comments and suggestions.

to this condition appeared in the literature as a classic statistical assumption that restricts the asymptotic behavior of the unknown function, and derives from a classical assumption on relative likelihoods. In De Groot (2004) the condition is denoted SP_4, and it compares the likelihood of bounded and unbounded sets. A simple interpretation for this condition is that, no matter how small is a set $B \succ \emptyset$, *it is impossible for every infinite interval* (n, ∞) *to be as least as likely as* B.[3] In practical terms the condition requires that in an increasing sequence of unboudned sets, the sets become eventually less likely than *any* bounded set. To check the condition in practice, one examines the relative likelihood of any bounded set B and compares it with infinite sets of the form (n, ∞). Eventually for large enough n, the set B must be more likely than (n, ∞). As a practical example, any continuous *integrable* density function on the line $f : R^+ \to R$ defines a relative likelihood that satisfies this condition. And as shown below this condition eliminates *fat tails*.

In order to generalize the *NP* estimation problem as much as possible, we extend Assumption SP_4 which was originally defined only for *density functions*, to *any continuous unknown function* $f : R^+ \to R$. We show that when SP_4 is satisfied, the unknown function can be represented by a function in a Hilbert space and the *NP* estimator can be extended appropriately to R^+. But when assumption SP_4 fails, the situation is quite different. The estimator does not have appropriate asymptotic behavior at infinity. It appears that a classic statistical assumption holds the cards for extending *NP* estimation to unbounded sample spaces.

Exploring other areas of the literature, we find other assumptions that we proved to be equivalent to SP_4 and in that sense determinant for extending *NP* estimation to R^+. In decision theory one such assumption is the *Monotone Continuity Axiom* of Arrow (1970) and another is the *Insensitivity to Rare Events* see Chichilnisky (2000, 2006). In optimal growth models it is *Dictatorship of the Present* as defined in Chichilnisky (1996) and the classic work of Koopmans on "impatience". When the key assumptions fail the estimator does not converge. In all cases, the failure leads to purely finitely additive measures on R^+, and to distributions with *heavy tails*. Econometric results involving purely additive measures are still an open issue, which suggests the current limits of econometrics. We show here that they are directly connected with Kurt Godel's work on the *Limits of Mathematics* - which established in the 1940's that any logical system that is sufficiently complex - such as Mathematics - is either ambiguous or leads to contradictions. We are therefore encountering a general phenomenon on the limits of Mathematics.

Results extending *semi NP* estimation and *NP* estimation to infinite cases, dealing with separate but related issues, can be found e.g. in Blundell et al (2006), Stinchcombe (2002), and Chen (2005) among others. Other articles in the *NP* literature include Andrews (1991) and Newey (1997), both of which again assume a compact support for the regressor.

2. Hilbert spaces

The methodology we use here is *weighted* Hilbert spaces as defined in Chichilnisky (1976, 1977), two publications that introduced Hilbert Spaces in Economics.

These earlier results suggested the advantages of using Hilbert Spaces in econometrics, in particular for *NP* estimation.[4] The rationale is simple: *NP* estimation is by nature infinite dimensional, because when the forms of the functions in the true model are unknown, the most efficient use of the data is to allow the estimated functions (or the number of estimated parameters) to depend on the size of the sample, tending to infinity with the sample size.

This provides a natural infinite dimensional context for *NP* estimation. In this context, Hilbert spaces are a natural choice, because they are the closest analog to Euclidean space in infinite dimensions.

Bergstrom (1985) pointed out that there is a natural limitation for the use of Hilbert space on the real line R. Standard Hilbert spaces such as $L_2(R)$ require that the unknown function approaches zero at infinity, a somewhat unreasonable limitation to impose on the economic model as they exclude widely used functions such as constant, increasing and cyclical functions on the line. To overcome his objection I suggested using *weighted* Hilbert spaces since these impose weaker limiting requirement at infinity as shown below. Bergstrom's article (1985) acknowledged my contribution to NP estimation in Hilbert spaces, but it is restricted to bounded sample spaces: his results apply to L_2 spaces of functions defined on a bounded segment of the line, $[a,b] \subset R$.

Below we extend the original methodology in Bergstrom (1985) to *unbounded* sample spaces by using *weighted* Hilbert spaces as I originally proposed. In exploring the viability of the proofs, we run into an interesting dilemma. When the sample space is the entire positive real line, Hilbert space techniques *still* require additional conditions on the asymptotic behavior of the unknown function at infinity. In bounded sample spaces such as $[a,b]$ this problem did not arise, because the unknown are continuous, and therefore bounded and belong to the Hilbert space $L_2[a,b]$. But this is not the case when the sample space is the positive line R^+. A continuous real valued function on R^+ may not be bounded, and may not be in the space $L_2(R^+)$[5]. Therefore the Fourier series expansions that are used for defining the estimator may not converge. With unbounded sample spaces, additional statistical assumptions are needed for *NP* estimation.

Consider the problem of estimating an unknown function f on R^+, for example a capital accumulation path through time or a density function, which are standard non - linear *NP* estimation problems. The unknown density function may be continuous, but not a square integrable function on R^+ namely an element of $L_2(R^+)$. Since the *NP* estimator is defined by approximating values of the Fourier coefficients of the unknown function (Berhstrom 1985), when the Fourier coefficients of the estimator do not converge, the estimator itself fails to converge. A similar situation arises in general *NP* estimation problems where the unknown function may not have the asymptotic behavior needed to ensure the appropriate convergence. This illustrates the difficulties involved in extending *NP* estimation in Hilbert spaces from bounded to unbounded sample spaces.

The rest of this chapter focuses on statistical necessary and sufficient conditions needed for extending the results from bounded intervals to the positive line $R.^+$

3. Statistical assumptions and *NP* estimation

A brief summary of earlier work is as follows. Bergstrom's statistical assumptions (Bergstrom, 1985) require that the unknown function f be continuous and bounded *a.e.* on the sample space $[a,b] \in R.$[6] His *sample design* assumes *separate observations at equidistant points*. The number of parameters increases with the size of the sample space, and disturbances are not necessarily normal.

Bergstrom uses an *orthogonal series* in Hilbert space to derive *NP* properties and prove convergence theorems. The *series* is orthonormal in the Hilbert space rather than in the sample space, so the elements remain unchanged as the sample size increases. This series includes polynomials or any dense family of orthonormal functions in the Hilbert space.

An *estimator* $\hat{f}$ is defined in a simple and natural manner (Bergstrom 1985): the first M Fourier coefficients of the unknown function f are estimated relative to the orthonormal set. Estimates of the coefficients are obtained from the sample by ordinary least squares regression, setting the rest of the Fourier coefficients to zero. Bergstrom (1985) shows that $E\left[\int_a^b \{\hat{f}_{MN}(x) - f(x)\}dx\right]$ can be made arbitrarily small by a suitable choice of M and of N. He also defines an estimator $f_N^*(x)$ that is optimal for the sample size N, and shows that this converges in a given metric to $f(x)$ as $N \to \infty$. A third theorem shows how an optimal value of M^* is related to the Fourier coefficients and the mean square errors of their estimates obtained from regressions with various values of M, and provides the basis for an estimation procedure. A "stopping rule" is also provided for estimating the optimum value of the parameter which, for a given sample, provides the exact number of Fourier coefficients to be estimated. The definition of the estimator and the proofs of these results require that f be an element of a Hilbert space.

Unbounded sample spaces give rise to a different type of problem. To explain the problem and motivate the results we first explain why earlier work was restricted to bounded sample spaces.

4. Why bounded sample spaces?

When working in Hilbert spaces, there are good technical reasons for requiring that the sample space be *bounded*. For example, consider the typical Hilbert space of functions L_2, the space of *square integrable* measurable real valued functions. Bergstrom (Bergstrom, 1985) considered the space $L_2[a,b]$ of functions defined on the bounded segment $[a,b] \subset R$, where $[a,b]$ represents the sample space. As he points out, there is no need to assume anything further than continuity for the unknown function.[7] Every continuous unknown function on the segment $[a,b]$ is bounded and belongs to the Hilbert space $L_2[a,b]$.

However when the sample space is unbounded, such as R^+, the square integrability condition of being in $L_2(R^+)$ function imposes significantly more restrictions. For example, for continuous functions of bounded variation, it requires that the functions to be estimated have a well defined limit at infinity, such as $\lim_{t\to\infty} f(t) = 0$. This is not a reasonable restriction to impose on the unknown function, for example, if the function represents capital accumulation, which typically increases over time. The restriction on $\lim_{t\to\infty} f(t)$ eliminates also other standard cases, such as constant, increasing or cyclical functions.

In mathematical terms, an appropriate transformation of the line can alleviate the problem. This was the methodology introduced in Chichilnisky (1976 and 1977), the first publications to use Hilbert spaces in economics. I defined then a Hilbert space $L_2(R^+)$ with a 'weight function' $\overline{\gamma}(t)$ that defines a *finite* density measure for R^+.[8] In this case, square integrability requires far less, only that the product of the function times the weight function, $f(t)\overline{\gamma}(t)$, converges to zero at infinity, rather then the function $f(t)$ itself. This is a more reasonable assumption, which is asymptotically satisfied by the solutions in most optimal growth models, where there is well defined a 'discount' factor $\gamma > 1$. The solution I considered was the (weighted) Hilbert space $L_2(R^+, \gamma)$ of all measurable functions f for which the absolute value of the 'discounted' product $f(t)e^{-\gamma t}$ is square integrable, (Chichilnisky, 1976 and 1977). As

already stated this does not require $\lim_{t\to\infty} f(t) = 0$, and it includes bounded, increasing and cyclical real valued functions on R^+.[9] It is of course possible to include other weight functions as part of the methodology introduced in (Chichilnisky 1976, 1977), provided the weight functions are monotonically decreasing and therefore invertible, but the ones specified in Chichilnisky (1976 and 1977) are naturally associated with the models at hand. This solution is an improvement, but the condition that the unknown function belongs to a Hilbert space *still* poses asymptotic restrictions at infinity, which are considered below.
In the case of optimal growth models Chichilnisky (1977), the methodology of weighted Hilbert spaces is based on a transformation map induced by the model itself, its own 'discount factor' $\overline{\gamma} : R^+ \to [0,1)$, $\overline{\gamma}(t) = e^{-\gamma t}$. Under this transformation, the unbounded sample space R^+ is mapped into the bounded sample space $[0,1)$ where the original assumptions and results for bounded sample spaces can be re-interpreted appropriately in a bounded sample space. This is the route followed in this paper.
Before doing so, however, it seems worth discussing briefly a different methodology that has been suggested for *NP* estimation with unbounded sample spaces,[10] explaining why it may be less suitable.

5. Compactifying the sample space

A natural approach to extend *NP* estimation to unbounded sample spaces would be to compactify the sample space, and apply the existing results to the compactified space. For example, the compactification of the positive real line R^+ yields a space that is equivalent to a bounded interval $[a,b]$. To proceed with *NP* estimation, one needs to reinterpret every function $f : R^+ \to R$ as a function defined on the compactified space, $\widetilde{f} : \widetilde{R} \to R$. As we see below, this requires from the onset that the function f on R has a well-defined limiting behavior at infinity, namely $\lim_{t\to\infty} f(t) < \infty$. Otherwise, f cannot be extended to a function on the compactified space. To lift this constraint, Peter Phillips suggested that one could *estimate* (rather than assume) the behavior of the unknown function at infinity.[11] But in all cases, *some* limit must be assumed for the unknown function, which can be considered an unrealistic requirement. The following example shows why.
Consider the *Alexandroff one point compactification* of the real line R^+, which consists of 'adding' to the real numbers a point of infinity $\{\infty\}$, and defining the corresponding neighborhoods of infinity. This is a frequently used technique of compactification. A function f on the line R can be extended to a function on the compactified line but *only if* f has a well - defined limiting behavior at infinity, namely if there exists a well defined $\lim_{t\to\infty} f(t)$. This is not always possible nor a reasonable restriction to impose, for example, this requirement excludes all cyclical functions, for which $\lim_{t\to\infty} f(t)$ does not exist.
One can explore more general forms of compactification, such as the *Stone - Cech compactification* of the line $\widehat{R}$, the most general possible compactification of the real line.[12] $\widehat{R}$ is a well behaved Hausdorff space, and is a *universal compactifier* of R, which means that every other compactification of R is a subset of it. Any function $f : R \to R$ can be extended to a function on the compactified space, $\widehat{f} : \widehat{R} \to R$. However it is difficult to interpret Hilbert Spaces of functions defined on $\widehat{R}$, since these would be square integrable functions defined on ultrafilters rather than on real numbers. Such spaces do not have a natural interpretation.
To overcome these difficulties, in the following we use *weighted* Hilbert Spaces for NP estimation on unbounded samples spaces.

6. *NP* estimation on Weighted Hilbert spaces

Following Chichilnisky (1976), (1977) consider the sample space $R^+ = [0, \infty)$ with a standard σ field and a finite density or 'weight function' $\overline{\gamma} : R^+ \rightarrow [1, 0)$, $\overline{\gamma}(t) - e^{-\gamma t}$, $\gamma > 1$, $\int_{R^+} e^{-\gamma t} dt < \infty$. Define the weighted Hilbert space H_γ, also denoted H, consisting of all measurable and square integrable functions $g(.) : R^+ \rightarrow R$ with the weighted L_2 norm $\| \, . \, \|$

$$\| g \|_2 = \left(\int_{R^+} g^2(t) e^{-\gamma t} dt \right)^{1/2}$$

Observe that the space H contains the space of bounded measurable functions $L_\infty(R^+)$, and includes all periodic and constant functions, as well as many increasing functions.
The weight function $\overline{\gamma}$ induces a homeomorphism, namely a bi-continuous one to one and onto transformation, between the positive real line and the interval $[1, 0)$, $\overline{\gamma} : R^+ \rightarrow [0, 1), \overline{\gamma}(t) = e^{-\gamma t}$. In the following we use a modified homeomorphism $\delta : R^+ \rightarrow [0, 1)$ defined as $\delta(t) = 1 - \overline{\gamma}(t) \in [0, 1]$ to maintain the standard order of the line. The transformation δ allows us to translate Bergstrom's 1985 methodology, assumptions and notation, which are valid for $[0, 1]$, to the positive real line R^+. The following section interprets the statistical assumptions in Bergstrom (1985) for NP estimation in this new context, and introduces new statistical assumptions.

7. Statistical assumptions and results on R^+

We have a sample of N paired observations $(t_1, y_1) ..., (t_N, y_N)$ in which $t_1, ...t_N$ are non random positive real numbers whose values are fixed by the statistician and $y_1, ...y_N$ are random variables whose joint distribution depends on $t_1, ...t_N$. we may In particular it is assumed that $E(y_i) = f(\delta(t_i)) = f(x_i)$, $(i = 1, ..., N)$ where f is an unknown function, $\delta : R^+ \rightarrow [0, 1)$ is the one to one transformation defined above, and $x_i = \delta(t_i)$.
We are concerned with estimating an unknown function $g : R^+ \rightarrow R$ over the sample space R^+ or, equivalently, estimating the function f over the bounded interval $[0, 1)$ defined by $f(.) = (g \circ \delta^{-1})(.) = g(\delta^{-1}(.)) : [0, 1) \rightarrow R$. The model is precisely described by Assumptions 1 to 4 below, which are a transformed version of the Assumptions in Bergstrom (1985), section 2, p. 11. We also require a new statistical assumption, Assumption 3 below, which is needed due to the unbounded nature of our sample space[13].
Observe that, given the properties of the transformation map δ, it is statistically equivalent to work with the non random variables $t_1, ...t_N$ or, instead, with the *transformed* non random variables $x_1 = x_1(t_1) ... x_N = x_N(t_N)$. To simplify the comparison with Bergstrom's (1985) results, it seems best to use the latter variables when describing the statistical model:
Assumption 1: (Sampling assumption) The observable random variables $y_1, ...y_N$ are assumed to be generated by the equations

$$y_i = f(x_i) + u_i = f(\delta(t_i)) + u_i$$

where

$$x_i = a + \frac{b - a}{2N}$$

$$x_{i+1} = x_i + \frac{b - a}{N}, i = 1, ..., N - 1$$

a, b are constants $(1 \geqslant b > a \geqslant 0)$ and $u_1 ... u_N$ are unobservable random variables[14] satisfying the conditions:

$$E(u_i) = 0$$
$$E(u_i^2) = \sigma^2$$
$$E(u_i, u_j) = 0 \quad i \neq j, i = 1, ..., N.$$

Assumption 2: The unknown function $g : R^+ \to R$ is continuous or, equivalently, the 'transformed' function $f : [0,1) \to R$ defined by $f(.) = go\delta^{-1}(.) : [0,1) \to R$, is continuous.
When the domain of a function f - namely the sample space - is the closed bounded interval $[0,1]$ then, being continuous, f is bounded and $f \in L_2[0,1]$ as pointed out in Bergstrom (1985), p. 11. One may therefore apply Hilbert Spaces techniques for *NP* estimation.
In our case, the (transformed) function f is defined over the (half open) interval $[0,1)$. Under appropriate boundary conditions f can be extended to the closed interval $[0,1]$. Continuity over the closed bounded interval implies boundedness, and furthermore it ensures that $f \in L_2[0,1]$. But this is no longer true when the sample space is the positive real line R^+, or, equivalently, the transformed sample space is $\delta(R^+) = [0,1)$. A continuous function defined on R^+ may not be bounded, and may not belong to $L_2(R^+)$.[15] For the unbounded sample space R^+, we require the following additional statistical assumption on the unknown function:
Assumption 3: The unknown function $g : R^+ \to R$ is in the Hilbert Space H or, equivalently, the transformed function $f : [0,1) \to R$ can be extended to a continuous function $f : [0,1] \to R$.
Assumption 4: The countable set of continuous functions $\phi_1(x(t)), ..., \phi_N(x(t))$ is a complete orthonormal set in the space $L_2(R^+)$ of square integrable functions on R^+ with ordinary Lebesgue measure μ.
This requires that the functions ϕ_j be continuous, linearly independent, dense in $L_2(R^+)$ and satisfy the conditions

$$\int_0^1 \phi_j^2(x)dx = 1, \ (j = 1, 2, ...)$$

and

$$\int_0^1 \phi_j(x).\phi_i(x)dx = 0, \ (j \neq i; j, i = 1, 2...).$$

Observe that one can consider different orthonormal sets, for example, (Bergstrom, 1985) considers an orthonormal set consisting of polynomials on increasing order.
On the basis of these Assumptions (1, 2, 3 and 4) the following results, which are reproduced from Bergstrom, 1985, obtain directly from those of Bergstrom, 1985. These results are expressed in the transformed unknown function $f : [0,1] \to R$ to facilitate comparison with Bergstrom (1985) but can be equivalently expressed on the unknown function $g : R^+ \to R$:

Theorem 1. *(Bergstrom, 1985) Let* $\hat{f}_{MN}(x)$ *be defined by*

$$\hat{f}_{MN}(x) = \hat{c}_1(M,N)\phi_1(x) + ... + \hat{c}_M(M,N)\phi_M(x) \quad (1)$$

where

$$\hat{c}_1(M,N)\phi_1(x), ..., \hat{c}_M(M,N)\phi_M(x)$$

are the values of

$$c_1, c_2, ..., c_M$$

that minimize

$$\sum_{i=1}^{N}\{y_1 - c_1\phi_1(x) - ... - c_M\phi_M(x)\}^2$$

i.e. there are sample regression coefficients. Then for an arbitrarily small real number $\varepsilon > 0$, *there are* M_ε *and* $N_\varepsilon(M)$ *such that*

$$E[\int_a^b \hat{f}_{MN}(x) - f(x)dx] < \varepsilon$$

if $M > M_\varepsilon$ *and* $N > N_\varepsilon(M)$.

Theorem 2. *(Bergstrom, 1985) Let* M^* *be the smallest integer such that*

$$E\left[\int_0^1 \{\widehat{f}_{M^*N}(x) - f(x)\}^2\right] \leq E\left[\int_0^1 \{\widehat{f}_{MN}(x) - f(x)\}^2\right] \quad (M = 1, ..., N)$$

where $\widehat{f}_{MN}(x)$ *is defined by (1) and let* $f_N^*(x)$ *be defined by*

$$f_N^*(x) = \widehat{f}_{M^*N}(x).$$

Then under Assumptions 1-4,

$$\lim_{N\to\infty}\left[\int_0^1 \{f_N^*(x) - f(x)\}^2 dx\right] = 0.$$

Definition 3. *Let* $c_1, ..., c_n, ...$ *be the Fourier coefficients of* $f(x)$ *relative to the orthonormal set* $\phi_1, ..., \phi_n$ *in the transformed set* $[0,1]$, *namely*

$$c_j = \int_0^1 f(x)\phi_j(x)dx, \quad (j = 1, 2, ...).$$

Observe that under the conditions the set $\phi_1, ..., \phi_n$ is orthonormal and therefore complete in $L_2[0,1]$ so that

$$\lim_{M\to\infty}\int_0^1 \{f(x) - \sum_{j=1}^{M} c_j\phi_j(x)\}^2 = 0,$$

and Parseval's inequality is satisfied (Kolmogorov, 1961, p. 98)

$$\int_0^1 f^2(x)dx = \sum_{j=1}^{\infty} c_j^2.$$

Theorem 4. *(Bergstrom 1985) Under Assumptions 1-4,*

$$\sum_{j=M+1}^{M^*} c_j^2 \geq \sum_{j=1}^{M^*} E(\widehat{c}_j(M^*, N) - c_j)^2 - \sum_{j=1}^{M} E(\widehat{c}_j(M, N) - c_j)^2 \quad (M = 1, ..., M^* - 1)$$

$$\sum_{j=M^*+1}^{M} c_j^2 \leqslant \sum_{j=1}^{M} E(\widehat{c}_j(M, N) - c_j)^2 - \sum_{j=1}^{M^*} E(\widehat{c}_j(M^*, N) - c_j)^2 \quad (M = M^* + 1, ..., N)$$

From the definition of the transformation δ and Assumptions 1 to 4, the proofs for the theorems above follow directly from Theorems 1, 2 and 3 in Bergstrom 1985..
Theorems 1, 2 and 4 are quite general, but the underlying assumptions (1 to 4) still require interpretation for the case of unbounded sample spaces. The following section tackles this issue.

8. Statistical assumptions on R^+

Assumptions 1, 2 and 4 have a ready interpretation in the transformed sample space. Assumption 3 is however of a different nature. It requires that the unknown function $g : R^+ \to R$ be an element of a (weighted) Hilbert space or, equivalently, that the transformed unknown function $f : [0,1) \to R$ can be extended to a continuous function in the Hilbert space $L_2[0,1]$. This condition is critical: when Assumption 3 is satisfied Theorems 1, 2 and 4 extend NP estimation to R^+, but otherwise these theorems, which depend on the properties of L_2 functions and the convergence of their Fourier coefficients, no longer work. What conditions are needed to ensure that Assumption 3 holds?[16] The following provides classical statistical conditions involving *relative likelihoods* (cf. De Groot, 2004, Chapter 6).

Theorem 5. *If a relative likelihood $\preceq$ satisfies assumptions SP_1 to SP_5 of De Groot (2004) Chapter 6, then there exists a probability function $f : R^+ \to R$ representing the relative likelihood $\preceq$ where f is an element of the Hilbert space $L_2(R^+)$ and Assumption 3 above is satisfied.*

Proof: Consider the five assumptions $SP_1, ..., SP_5$ provided in Degroot (2004) Chapter 6. Together they imply the existence of a countably additive probability measure on R^+ that agrees with the relative likelihood order $\gtrsim$ (cf. Degroot, 2004), Section 6.4, p. 76-77). Given any countably additive measure μ on R one can always find a functional representation as a measurable function, $f : R^+ \to R$, that is integrable, $f \in L_1(R^+)$ and satisfying $\mu(A) = \int_A f(x)dx$ (Yosida 1952). In other words, the five assumptions $SP_1, ..., SP_5$ guarantee the existence of an absolutely continuous distribution representing the 'relative likelihood of events' (Degroot, 2004).
Since the space of integrable functions on the (positive) real line is contained in the space of square integrable functions on the (positive) real line, $L_1(R^+) \subset L_2(R^+)$ (Yosida, 1952) it follows, under the assumptions, that $f \in L_2(R^+)$ as we wished to prove. Thus the five statistical assumptions of Degroot (2004) suffice to guarantee our Assumption 3, and hence the results of Theorems 1, 2 and 4.■
Among the five fundamental statistical assumptions of Degroot (2004) there is one, SP_4, which plays a key role: it is necessary and sufficient to extend the NP estimation results to unknown density functions on R^+.The next step is to define assumption SP_4 and explain its role. The notation $A \succeq B$ indicates that the likelihood of the set or event A is higher than the likelihood of B, see Degroot (2004).

Definition 6. ***Assumption*** *SP_4 (De Groot 2004)*: Let $A_1 \supset A_2 \supset$ ...be a decreasing sequence of events, and B some fixed event such that $A_i \succsim B$ for $i = 1,2....$, Then $\bigcap_{i=1}^{\infty} A_i \gtrsim B_i$.

To clarify the role of SP_4, suppose that each infinite interval of the form $(n, \infty) \subset R, n = 1,2,...$ is regarded as more likely (by the relative likelihood) than some fixed small subset B of R. Since the intersection of all these intervals is empty, B must be equivalent to the empty set ϕ. In other words, if B is more likely than the empty set, $B \succ \phi$, then regardless of how small is

B is, it is impossible for every infinite interval (n, ∞) to be as likely as B. One way to interpret the role of Assumption SP_4 is in averting 'heavy tails':

Definition 7. *We say that a relative likelihood $\succsim$ has 'heavy tails' when for any given set B, there exist an $N > 0$ such that $n > N$ and $C \supset (n, \infty)$, $C \succsim B$ namely C is as likely as $B \subset R^+$.*[17]

Intuitively, this definition states that there exist infinite intervals or 'tail sets' of the form (n, ∞) with arbitrarily large measure, which may be interpreted as 'heavy tails'.

Theorem 8. *When assumption SP_4 fails, relative likelihoods have 'heavy tails'.*

Proof: The logical negation of SP_4 implies that there exists a large enough n such that (n, ∞) is as likely than B, for any bounded B. This implies that the probability measure of the event (n, ∞) does not go to zero when n goes to infinity. Therefore, one obtains 'heavy tails' as defined above.■

It is possible to interpret SP_4 to apply to any unknown function $f : R^+ \to R$ within the statistical model defined above. For this one must reinterpret the relationship $\preceq$ that appears in the definition of SP_4 as follows:

Definition 9. Let $f : R^+ \to R$ be a continuous positive valued function. Then the expression $A \preceq B$ *means* $\int_A f dx < \int_B f dx$, where integration is with respect to the standard measure on R^+.[1]

When working in Hilbert spaces, we use a similar definition of the expression $\preceq$ to obtain necessary and sufficient conditions below:

Definition 10. Let $f : R^+ \to R$ be a continuous function. Then the expression $A \preceq B$ *means* $\int_A f^2 dx < \int_B f^2 dx$, where integration is with respect to the standard measure on R^+.[18]

The following extends SP_4 to any continuous function f: $R^+ \to R$:

Definition 11. Assumption SP_4 in Hilbert spaces. Let $A_1 \supset A_2 \supset$ ...be a decreasing sequence of sets in R^+, and B some fixed set such that $A_i \succsim B$, namely $\int_{A_i} f^2(x)dx > \int_B f^2(x)dx$ for $i = 1, 2....$,then $\bigcap_{i=1}^{\infty} A_i \gtrsim B_i$.

In other words, if B is any set such that $\int_B f^2(x)dx > 0$, then regardless of how small is B, it is impossible for every infinite interval (n, ∞) to satisfy $\int_{(n,\infty)} f^2(x)dx > \int_B f^2(x)dx$. This is a reasonable extension of SP_4 provided above.

9. *SP4* is necessary and sufficient for extending *NP* estimation to R^+

To obtain specific necessary and sufficient conditions for NP estimation, consider now the statistical model defined above, and assume that all the statistical assumptions of Bergstrom (1985) are satisfied, namely Assumptions 1, 2 and 4. We study the estimation of an unknown function $g : R^+ \to R$. When the model is restricted to the bounded sample space $[0, 1]$, namely $g : [0, 1] \to R$, Theorems 1, 2 and 4 of Bergstrom (1985) ensure the existence of an *NP* estimator in Hilbert spaces with the appropriate asymptotic behavior. The following provides a necessary and sufficient condition for extending the NP estimation results from the sample space $[0, 1]$ to the unbounded sample space R^+ :

[1] Observe that this interpretation of the relationship $\preceq$ is identical the definition of relative likelihood when f is a density function. Therefore it agrees with the definition provided in the previous section.

Theorem 12. *Assumption SP_4 of De Groot (2004), as extended above, is necessary and sufficient for extending NP estimation in Hilbert Spaces from the sample space [0,1] to the unbounded sample space R^+.*

Proof: This follows directly from Theorems 1, 2, 4, 5 and 8 above. ■
Observe that when SP_4 fails, the distribution induced by the density f is not countably additive and cannot be represented by a function in H, and the estimator, which is constructed from Fourier coefficients, fails to converge.

10. Connection with decision theory

The general applicability of *NP* estimation, and the central role played by assumption SP_4, make it desirable to situate the results in the context of the larger literature. A natural connection that comes to mind is *decision theory.* There is an logical parallel between the classic assumptions on relative likelihood (De Groot, 2004) and the classic axioms of decision making under uncertainty (Arrow, 1970). From assumptions on relative likelihood one obtains probability measures that represent the likelihood of events. From the axioms of decision making under uncertainty, one derives subjective probability measures that define expected utility. One would expect to find an axiom in the foundations of choice under uncertainty that corresponds to assumption SP_4 on relative utility. Such an axiom exists: it is called *Monotone Continuity* in Arrow (1970) and as shown below, it is equivalent to SP_4. We use standard definitions for *actions* and *lotteries* used in the theory of choice under uncertainty, see e.g. Arrow (1970) and Chichilnisky (2000).

Definition 13. A vanishing sequence *of sets in the real line R is a family of of sets* $\{A_i\}_{i=1,....} \subset R^+$ *satisfying* $A_1 \supset A_2 \supset ... \supset A_i ...,$*and* $\bigcap_{i=1}^{\infty} A_i = \phi$.

Definition 14. *The expression $A \succ B$ is used to indicate that action $A \subset R$ is 'preferred' to action $B \subset R$.*

Definition 15. *Monotone Continuity Axiom (MCA, Arrow (1970)) Given two actions A and B where $A \succ B$ and a vanishing sequence $\{E_i\}$, suppose that $\{A_i\}$ and $\{B_i\}$ yield the same consequences as A and B on E_i^c and any arbitrary consequence c on E_i. Then for all i sufficiently large, $A_i \succ B_i$.*

The following results use the identification see Yosida (1952, 1974), , Chichilnisky (2000) of a distribution on the line R with a continuous linear real valued function defined on the space of bounded functions on the line, $L_\infty(R)$.[19]

Theorem 16. *Assumption SP_4 of De Groot (2004) is equivalent to the Monotone Continuity Axiom (1970).*

Proof: The strategy is to show that SP_4 and the Monotone Continuity Axiom (MCA) are each necessary and sufficient for the existence of a ranking of events $\preceq$ in R^+ (by relative likelihood, or by choice, respectively) that is representable by an integrable function on R^+.[20] Consider first the Monotone Continuity Axiom (MCA). Chichilnisky (2006) showed it is necessary and sufficient for the existence of a choice function that is a continuous linear function on R, an element of the dual space $L_\infty^*(R)$, represented by a countably additive measure on R and thus admitting a representation by an integrable function in $L_1(R)$. The argument is as follows: the dual space $L_\infty^*(R)$ is (by definition) the space of all continuous linear real valued functions on $L_\infty(R^+)$. It has been shown that this space consists (Yosida, 1952, 1974) of both countably additive and purely finitely additive measures on R. Chichilnisky (2006) showed Monotone Continuity Axiom rules out purely finitely additive linear measures and ensures that the choice criterion is represented by a countably additive measure on R, Theorem 2 of Chichilnisky (2006). Since a countably additive measure on R can always be represented by an integrable function in $L_1(R^+)$ (Yosida, 1952, 1974), this completes the first part of the proof. Consider now SP_4. De Groot De Groot (2004) showed that Assumption SP_4 eliminates distributions that are purely finitely additive, as shown in para. 3, page 73 Section 6.2 of De Groot (2004), ensuring that the distribution is represented by a countably additive measure, which completes the proof.■

11. Rare events and sustainability

When estimating an unknown path f over time, SP_4 can be interpreted as a condition on the behavior of the unknown function on finite and infinite time intervals. A related necessary and sufficient condition has been used in the literature on Sustainable Development: it is called *Dictatorship of the Present*, Chichilnisky (1996). For any order $\preceq$ of continuous bounded paths $f : R^+ \to R$:

Definition 17. *We say that $\preceq$ is a Dictatorship of the Present when for any two f and g there exists an $N = N(f,g)$ such that $f \preceq g \Leftrightarrow f' \preceq g'$, for any f' and g' that are identical to f and g on the interval $[0, N)$.*

The condition of dictatorship of the present Chichilnisky (1996) is equivalent to the representation of a welfare criterion by countably additive measures, and by an attendant integrable function on the line. The condition is also logically identical to Insensitivity to Rare Events Chichilnisky (2000, 2006), when the numbers in the real line R^+ represents events rather than time periods:

Definition 18. *(Chichilnisky (2000, 2006)) A ranking of lotteries $W : L \to R$ is called Insensitive to Rare Events when for any two lotteries, f and g, there is an $\varepsilon > 0, \varepsilon = \varepsilon(f,g)$ such that $W(f) > W(g) \Leftrightarrow W(f') > W(g')$ for every f' and g' that differ from f and g solely on sets of measure smaller than ε.*

Definition 19. *(Chichilnisky 2000, 2006) A ranking of lotteries $W : L \to R$ is Sensitive to Rare Events when it is not Insensitive to Rare Events.*

Theorem 20. *Assumption SP_4 is equivalent to Monotone Continuity and to Insensitivity for Rare Events, and the latter is logically identical to Dictatorship of the Present. In their appropriate contexts, each of the four conditions (SP_4, Monotone Continuity, Insensitivity for Rare Events, and Dictatorship of the Present) is necessary and sufficient for extending NP estimation results to R^+.*

Proof: Chichilnisky (2006) established that *Insensitivity to Rare Events* is equivalent to the *Monotone Continuity Axiom* (MCA) in Arrow (1970), cf. Theorem 2 in Chichilnisky (2006). Chichilnisky (1996, 2000) showed that *Insensitivity to Rare Events* is logically identical to *Dictatorship of the Present*. Theorems 12 and 16 complete the proof of the theorem.■

12. K. Godel and the limits of mathematics

The critical condition that allows extending econometric estimation from bounded domains to the entire line is the logical negation of purely finitely additive measures, as was shown in the previous Section. The constructibility of purely finite measures has been shown in turn to be equivalent to the existence of "ultrafilters", to Hahn Banach's theorem and the Axiom of Choice in Mathematics, Chichilnisky (2009, 2010a, 2010b). Furthermore, the Axiom of Choice was established by K. Godel early on to be independent from the other axioms of Mathematics (Godel (1943)), so there is a formulation of Mathematics with the Axiom of Choice and another without it, both are equally valid. This Axiom of Choice itself is therefore an unprovable proposition from the other axioms of Mathematics - thus providing a link with the ambiguity feature of large logical systems that was first identified by K. Godel last century (1943). Equally the two separate and distinct mathematical systems - one with and the other without the Axiom of Choice – are equally valid and they are contradictory with each other. Therefore there exist mathematically and logically correct statements that are contradictory within the classic body of Mathematics. These statements confirm K. Godel's incompleteness theorem for Mathematics.

More precisely, the formal equivalence we are seeking between the results of this chapter and the Limits of Mathematics, has been established in the previous Section of this chapter, where a link was established to Chichilnisky's axiom of "Sensitivity to Rare Events" - which, in Chichilnisky (2009, 2010a, 2010b, 2011), was proven to be identical with the negation of the Axiom of Choice.

The literature on the Limits of Mathematics that was initiated by Godel, is deeply connected therefore with the results on the Limits of Econometrics presented in this chapter.

13. Conclusions

We extended Bergstrom's 1985 results on *NP* estimation in Hilbert spaces to unbounded sample sets, using previous results in Chichilnisky (1976 and 1977). The focus was on the statistical assumptions needed for the extension. When estimating an unknown function on the positive line R^+, we obtained a necessary and sufficient condition that derives from a classic assumption on relative likelihoods, SP_4 *in* De Groot (2004).We extended assumption SP_4 , and therefore the results, to any unknown continuous function $f : R^+ \to R$. We also showed that the SP_4 assumption is equivalent to well known axioms for choice under uncertainty, such as the *Monotone Continuity Axiom* in Arrow (1970), *Insensitivity to Rare Events* in Chichilnisky (2000, 2006), and to criteria used for sustainable choice over time, such as *Dictatorship of the Present* (1996).

When the key assumptions fail, the estimators on bounded sample spaces that are based on Fourier coefficients, do not converge. We showed that this involves 'heavy tails' and purely finitely additive measures, thus suggesting a limit to *NP* econometrics.

14. Footnotes

1. In 1980 Rex Bergstrom and I discussed Hilbert spaces at a Colchester pub at a time he offered me the Keynes Chair of Economics at the University of Essex, which I accepted. Bergstrom was interested in my recent work introducing Hilbert and Sobolev Spaces in Economics (Chichilnisky, 1976, 1977) and I suggested that Hilbert Spaces were a natural space to use in *NP* Econometrics, which apparently inspired his 1985 chapter. Bergstrom passed away in 2006, and his former student Peter Phillips organized this conference in his honor. This paper is in honor of a great man, and attempts to complete a conversation between us that was left pending for 27 years.

2. In a *weighted* Hilbert space the real line R is endowed with a finite density function, such as e^{-t}, rather than the standard uniform measure on R.
3. See p. 73, Section 6.2 of De Groot (2004), para. 4 following Assumption SP_4.
4. *NP* estimation in Hilbert Spaces was very interesting to me at the time, as I had introduced Hilbert spaces in economic models in a PhD dissertation with Gerard Debreu at UC Berkeley (Chichilnisky 1976) and in a neoclassical optimal growth model (Chichilnisky 1977), including L_2, weighted L_2 and Sobolev spaces. A few years later, in 1981, Gallant (1981) used again Sobolev norms for non - parametric estimation.
5. The same problem arises when the sample space is bounded but not closed, such as $[a, b)$.
6. This implies that the estimator f is in the Hilbert Space L_2 of square integrable functions denoted $L_2[a, b]$, which is the space of measurable functions $f : [a, b] \to R$ satisfying $\int_a^b \mid f(x) \mid^2 dx < \infty$.
7. Bergstrom (1985) required the function to be continuous *a.e.* on $[a, b]$ which is essentially the same in our case.
8. The weighted Hilbert space H is defined as the space of all square integrable functions on the positive line using the (finite) density function δ^{-x} : a function $f \in H$ when the 'weighted' integral $\int_{R^+} \mid f(x)\delta^{-x} \mid^2 dx < \infty$.
9. This weaker assumption always works, but has no natural interpretation when the model lacks a 'discount factor'.
10. Private communication with Peter Phillips.
11. Private communication.
12. This can be described as the space of all *ultrafilters* of the real line R.
13. And the fact that [0,1) is not compact.
14. To simplify notation we may assume in the following without loss of generality $a = 0$, $b = 1$.
15. Appropriate boundary conditions are needed for this to be the case, for example, in the case of continuous functions of bounded variation,
$\lim_{x \to \infty} f(x) = 0$.
16. Since we consider weight functions $\overline{\gamma}$ one could interpret the requirement simply as the fact that g^2 does not go to infinity "too fast". But what does "too fast" mean in a non parametric context? Compared to what? Imposing a limiting condition at infinity or at a boundary $(x \to 1)$ becomes a parametric requirement that conflicts with the intention of non-parametric estimation.Alternatively one could choose another "weighting" function $\widehat{\gamma}$ on the definition of H_γ for which $g \in H_\gamma$, but this becomes an arbitrary parameter and defeats the "non parametric" nature of the problem. When estimating a density function f over R^+ one may answer the question by reference to the properties of the associated relative likelihood function (**?**), or, when estimating an investment path over time, one may consider the behavior of the associated capital accumulation path. A referee pointed out that an alternative choice of weighting function is the density of the regressor (assuming it has one). In practice this is not known but could be estimated. If one uses the empirical cdf, $\widehat{\Pi}(t) = \sum_i I\{t_i \leqslant t\}/N$, then $x_i = \widehat{\Pi}^{-1}(t_i) = (i-1)/N$. $\widehat{\Pi}$ is not invertible in a strict sense, but this can be handled using a kernel-smoothed version of it. Using the density $\pi(t) = \Pi'(t)$, the central condition becomes $\int_{R_+} g^2(x)\pi(t)dt = E\{g^2(t)\} < \infty$ and highlights that the condition concerns both the regression function and the distribution / transformation of the random valiable t.

17. Other definitions of the phenomenon known as 'heavy tails' exist, and are not discussed here. Our interpretation is presented as one possible definition of heavy tails that is justified by the fact that it is based only on the 'primitives' of the statistical theory namely, on 'relative likelihoods'.
18. Observe that the interpretation of the relationship $\preceq$ is identical to the definition of relative likelihood when f is a density function. Therefore it agrees with the definition provided in the previous section.
19. Namely an element of the dual space of $L_\infty(R)$, denoted $L_\infty^*(R)$.
20. Namely a function in $L_1(R^+)$

15. References

[1] Andrews, D. "Asymptotic Normality of Series Estimators for Nonparametric and Semiparametric Regression Models" *Econometrica*, 59, 307-345, 1991.

[2] Arrow, K. *Essays in the Theory of Risk Bearing*, Amsterdam and Oxford: North Holland (1970).

[3] Bergstrom, R. "The Estimation of Non Parametric Functions in a Hilbert Space", *Econ. Theory*, 1, 7-26, 1985.

[4] Blundell, R. X. Chen and D. Kristensen, "Semi-nonparametric IV estimation of shape invariant Engel curves" Working Paper Columbia University, 2006.

[5] Chen, X. Hansen, L.P. and Sheinkman, J. "Principal Components and the Long Run", Working Paper, October 2000, revised November 2005.

[6] Chichilnisky, G. *Manifolds of Preferences and Equilibria*, PhD dissertation UC Berkeley, 1976

[7] Chichilnisky, G. "Non Linear Functional Analysis and Optimal Economic Growth", *J. Math Analysis and Applications*, Vol 61, No 2, Nov 15, 1977 p. 504-520.

[8] Chichilnisky, G. "An Axiomatic Approach to Sustainable Development" *Social Choice and Welfare*, 3, No 2, p. 231-257, 1996.

[9] Chichilnisky, G. "An Axiomatic Approach to Choice Under Uncertainty with Cataastrophic Risks" in *Topology and Markets*, Fields Institute of Mathematical Sciences, Toronto, Canada, 1996, American Mathematical Society ISSN 1968 5265;22 Providence Rhode Island, 02940 and *Resource and Energy Economics*, 2000. Also *Encyclopedia of Environmetrics*, 2002

[10] Chichilnisky, G. "The Topology of Fear" *Journal of Mathematical Economics*, 2009 - based on Columbia University Working Papaer, presented at 2006 NBER GE Conference in Honor of Gerard Debreu, UC Berkeley, California, September 2006.

[11] Chichilnisky, G. "The Foundation of Probability with Black Swans" *Mathematical Social Sciences*, 2010

[12] Chichilnisky, G. "The Foundation of Statistics with Black Swans" *Journal of Probability and Statistics*, 2011

[13] Chichilnisky, G."Catastrophic Risks with Finite or Infinite States" *International Jounral of Ecological Economics*, March 2011.

[14] Chichilnisky "Sustainable Markets with Short Sales" *Economic Theory*, 2011, in press.

[15] Chichilnisky, G. "Non Parametric Estimation in Hilbert Spaces" *Econometric Theory* 2010, Invited Address at Conference in Honor of Rex Bergstrom, (P. Philips) Colchester, Essex, UK, May 2006.

[16] De Groot, M. *Optimal Statistical Decisions*, John Wiley and Sons, Wiley Classics Library, Hoboken, New Jersey, 2004
[17] Gallant, A.R. "On the bias of flexible functional forms" *J. of Econometrics*, 15, 1981, p. 211-246.
[18] Newey, W.K. "Convergence Rates and Asymptotic Normality for Series Estimators" *Journal of Econometrics*, 79, 147-168, 1997.
[19] Kolmogorov, A.N. and Fomin, S.V. 1961, *Elements of the theory of Functions and Functional Analysis*, 2, New York: Graylock Press.
[20] Priestley M.B. and Chao M.T: "Non parametric Function Fitting", *J. Royal Stat. Society*, 1972.
[21] Stinchcombe, M. "Some Genericity Analysis in Nonparametric Statistics", Working Paper, December 10, 2002.
[22] Yosida, K. *Funcional Analysis* 1974 4th edition, New York Heidelberg: Springer Verlag
[23] Yosida, K. and E. Hewitt, 1952 "Finitely Level Independent Measures", *Transactions of the American Math. Society*, 72, 46-66.

2

Instrument Generating Function and Analysis of Persistent Economic Times Series: Theory and Application

Tsung-wu Ho
Dept. of Finance, Shih Hsin University
Taiwan, R.O.C.

1. Introduction

The traditional approach to the persistence properties of time series is unit root tests, and because of the near unit root bias, the median-unbiased procedure of Andrews (1993) is widely used. In this article, we show that: To calculate half life from AR(1), the instrument generating function estimator of Phillips *et al.* (2004) is not only an asymptotically normal estimator, but also an easy-to-use alternative to Andrews (1993); to calculate half life from AR(p), we propose a FM-AR model, which is a modified version of Phillips' (1995) FM-VAR.

There are two approaches to study the persistence/convergence property of a univariate time series, for example, real exchange rate: unit root test and half life. The unit root approach to the persistence properties models the series either as trend-stationary, where innovations have no permanent effects, or difference stationary, implying that shocks have permanent effects[1]. However, reliance on unit root tests does not provide a measure of uncertainty of the estimates of finiteness or permanence of innovations because a rejection of the unit root null could still be consistent with a stationary process with highly persistent shocks. In addition, an important pitfall in using the autoregressive (AR, thereafter) model to analyze the persistence of shocks to the data is that standard estimators, such as least squares, are significantly *downwardly biased* in finite samples, especially when the true autoregressive parameter is close to but less than one. Problem of *near-unit root bias* biases empirical results in favor of stationarity.

Let y denote the log of real exchange rate, the estimation of half life begins with the autoregression below

$$y_t = \alpha y_{t-1} + u_t, \tag{1}$$

This model is the same as that used for testing whether there is a unit root in a time series—consequently, this model is often referred to as the Dickey–Fuller regression. The half-life of shocks, which is the time it takes for a unit shock to dissipate by 50%, is calculated from the AR parameter α, the formal definition is:

---

[1] For example, Papell (1997).

$$\text{Half Life} = \begin{cases} \dfrac{\ln(0.5)}{\ln(\rho)}, & \text{if } 0 < \rho < 1 \\ \infty, & \text{if } \rho \geq 1 \end{cases}$$

Empirically, to compute half-life, one has to estimate coefficient α of (1), one problem of estimation is *near-unit root bias*, which biases empirical results in favor of finding stationarity. That is, standard estimators, such as least squares, are significantly *downwardly biased* in finite samples, especially when the true autoregressive parameter is close to but less than one. In this case, the process is close to being non-stationary and, as the LS estimator minimizes the regression residual variance, it will tend to make the data-generating process appear to be more stationary than it actually is by forcing the AR parameter away from unity.

As lower values of the AR parameter imply faster speeds of adjustment following a shock, this will also result in a downward bias to LS-based estimates of half-lives of shocks. In addition to the inherent difficulties in distinguishing between the stationary and random walk processes for the real interest rate.

In a nutshell, conventional procedure estimates α to characterize the persistence of time series has two main disadvantages: (i) the least squares estimates of the AR parameter in unit root regressions will be biased toward zero in small samples (Orcutt, 1948); and (ii) they have low power against plausible trend stationary alternatives (DeJong *et al.*, 1992). The downward bias in LS estimates of the AR parameter arises because there is an asymmetry in the distribution of estimators of the AR parameter in AR models (the distribution is skewed to the left, resulting in the median exceeding the mean). As a result, the median is a better measure of central tendency than the mean in least squares estimates of AR models.

The median-unbiased procedure proposed by Andrews (1993) and Andrews and Chen (1994) is usually suggested in literature to estimate (1), which combines unbiasedness with the use of point and interval estimators in achieving a more accurate estimate of the persistence of shocks to economic time series. Andrews' (1993) median unbiased estimator (MU thereafter) uses a bias correction method which delivers an impartiality property to the decision making process because there is an equal chance of under- or over- estimating the AR parameter in the unit root regression. MU is widely used in empirical studies. For example, Murray and Papell (2002), Cashin *et al.* (2004), Sekioua(2008), and Cerrato *et al* (2008). However, as mentioned by Andrews (1993), MU is merely an unbiased model selection procedure without asymptotic theory, where there lacks an explicit optimality property for it; that is, we do not know whether it is a best MU estimator. It is possible that the estimator does not fully exploit all the information in the sufficient statistics for the parameters. More importantly, the construction of confidence intervals for MU is not an easy-to-use procedure.

Recently, Phillips *et al.* (2004) proposed an instrument generating function(IGF thereafter) estimator to estimate (1), which is also an *asymptotically median unbiased* estimator and can be used to produce symmetric confidence intervals, and it has no problem of discontinuity in the confidence intervals in the transition from stationary to nonstationary cases, which also yields a *t*-ratio that has a standard normal distribution when $\alpha=1$, as well as when $|\alpha|<1$. This enables us to construct the confidence intervals in a conventional way easily.

In contrast to this stark dichotomy between whether shocks to the series are mean reverting (finite persistence) or not (permanent), this paper characterizes the extent of reversion by applying the nonlinear instruments generating function (IGF thereafter) method, proposed by Phillips *et al.* (2004), to measure the estimates of the *half-life* of shocks to the series. Like AMU, the IGF estimator of Phillips *et al.* (2004) removes the downward bias of standard LS estimators. Moreover, the IGF based confidence intervals have slightly smaller coverage probabilities than AMU, and the *t*-statistic is distributed as standard normal distribution asymptotically.

Point and interval estimators are useful statistics for providing information to draw conclusions about the duration of shocks, unlike hypothesis testing, they are informative when a hypothesis is not rejected. Because the IGF estimator is shown to be asymptotically standard normal, the construction of confidence intervals is very straightforward.

For AR(p) model, impulse-response approach is used, typical examples are Murray and Papell (2002) and Sekioua (2008). To further the study, based upon the FM asymptotics of Phillips (1995), we propose a FM-AR to directly estimate the coefficients of any AR(p) process.

2. The Econometric methodology

2.1 IGF estimator for DF-AR(1)

Phillips *et al.* (2004) studies the properties of IGF estimator in which the instruments are nonlinear functions of integrated processes. Framework of Phillips *et al.* (2004) extends the analysis of So and Shin (1999)[2], providing a more general analysis of IV estimation in potentially nonstationary autoregressions and showing that the Cauchy estimator has an optimality property in the class of certain IV procedures.

For (1), Phillips *et al.* (2004) consider the IV estimator of α given by

$$\alpha = \frac{\sum_{t=1}^{n} F(y_{t-1}) y_t}{\sum_{t=1}^{n} F(Y_{t-1}) y_{t-1}} \tag{2}$$

Here, α is an IV estimator in which the instrument is generated by the IGF *F*. In its general form, the class of IV estimators that can be represented by (2) includes, of course, the conventional OLS estimator as a special case with the linear IGF $F(x) = x$. However, this paper will concentrate on IV estimators constructed with various nonlinear IGF's.

The bounded optimal IV estimator with asymptotic sign IGF has some nice properties that the conventional OLS estimator does not have. The estimator yields a *t*-ratio that has a standard normal limit distribution when α=1, as well as when $|\alpha|<1$. This enables us to construct and interpret the confidence interval for α in a conventional way. On the other hand, of course, the *t*-ratio based on the OLS estimator has a limit normal distribution only when $|\alpha|<1$ and its limit distribution is non-Gaussian when distribution has implications for tests of a unit root. These properties are explored in So and Shin (1999), where the Cauchy estimator was first suggested, Phillips *et al.* (2004) proposed six nonlinear instrument generating functions summarized below.

Because of singularity problem, in this article, we report the IVi3 results for our empirical study, where $F(y_{t-1})=y_{t-1}\text{Exp}(-|y_{t-1}|)$ is used for lagged level y_{t-1}. To control possible cross-

---

[2] In recent work, So and Shin (1999) suggested the use of the Cauchy estimator, which uses the sign function as an instrumental variable, in place of the ordinary least squares (OLS) estimator in autoregressions that included both stationary and nonstationary cases.

sectional dependency among currencies, we also follow Chang(2002) to insert a variable c such that $y_{t-1}\text{Exp}(-c|y_{t-1}|)$, and c is defined by

IV Estimators	Instrument generating functions, $F()$
IVh1	$\text{sgn}(y_{t-1})$
IVh2	$y_{t-1}\cdot\mathbf{I}\{\|y_{t-1}\|\le K\}+\text{sgn}(y_{t-1})K\cdot\mathbf{I}\{\|y_{t-1}\|>K\}$
IVh3	$\arctan(y_{t-1})$
IVi1	$\text{sgn}(y_{t-1})\cdot\mathbf{I}\{\|y_{t-1}\|\le K\}$
IVi2	$y_{t-1}\cdot\mathbf{I}\{\|y_{t-1}\|\le K\}$
IVi3	$y_{t-1}\text{Exp}(-\|y_{t-1}\|)$

$$c = \frac{K}{s(\Delta y_t)\sqrt{T}}$$

where $s(\Delta y_t)$ denotes the standard deviation of Δy_t, and K is a constant fixed at 3. In addition, the recursive de-meaning procedure[3] is also applied.

Using the 0.05 and 0.95 quantile functions of α estimate, we can construct two-sided 90% confidence intervals for the true α. These confidence intervals can be used either to provide a measure of the accuracy of α or to construct the conventional exact one- or two-sided tests of the null hypothesis that $\alpha = \alpha_0$. In this paper, we use such symmetric confidence intervals only to provide a measure of the accuracy of α estimate.

2.2 IGF estimator for ADF-AR(p)

In addition, the presence of serial correlation (typical in economic time series) means that (1) will often not be appropriate. In such cases, (1) is augmented to be an AR(p) model by adding lagged first-order difference. Hence, the starting point of this analysis is the following ADF regression:

$$y_t = \alpha y_{t-1} + \sum_{k=1}^{p} \delta_k \Delta y_{t-k} + \varepsilon_t \tag{3}$$

Similarly, (3) is estimated by IGF. For augmented differenced lagged variables, instruments are themselves without IGF transformation. Subsequently, we then define the matrices below

$$\mathbf{y} = \begin{pmatrix} y_{p_1} \\ \vdots \\ y_T \end{pmatrix}, \mathbf{y}_\ell = \begin{pmatrix} y_p \\ \vdots \\ y_{T-1} \end{pmatrix}, \mathbf{X} = \begin{pmatrix} x'_{p_1} \\ \vdots \\ x'_T \end{pmatrix}, \boldsymbol{\varepsilon} = \begin{pmatrix} \varepsilon_{p_1} \\ \vdots \\ \varepsilon_T \end{pmatrix}$$

where $x'_t = \left(\Delta y_{t-1}, \ldots\ldots \Delta y_{t-p}\right)$ collects the lagged difference terms. Then the augmented AR regression (3) can be written in matrix form as

[3] See eq.(25) in Phillips *et al.* (2004, p.231).

$$y = y_\ell \alpha + X\beta + \varepsilon = Y\gamma + \varepsilon \tag{4}$$

where $\beta = (\alpha_1, \dots\dots \alpha_p)'$, $Y = (y_\ell, X)$, and $\gamma = (\alpha, \beta')'$. For equation (4), IV estimator is constructed below

$$\hat{\gamma} = \begin{bmatrix} \hat{\alpha} \\ \beta \end{bmatrix} = \begin{bmatrix} F(y_\ell)'y_\ell & F(y_\ell)'X \\ X'y_\ell & X'X \end{bmatrix}^{-1} \begin{bmatrix} F(y_\ell)'y \\ X'y \end{bmatrix}$$

where $F(y_\ell) = \left(F(y_p), \cdots F(y_T)\right)'$.

Under the null, we have $\alpha - 1 = B_T^{-1} A_T$, where

$$\mathbf{A_T} = F(y_\ell)'\varepsilon - F(y_\ell)'X(X'X)^{-1}X'\varepsilon$$
$$= \sum_{t=1}^{T} F(y_{t-1})\varepsilon_t - \sum_{t=1}^{T} F(y_{t-1})x_t' \left(\sum_{t=1}^{T} x_t x_t' \right)^{-1} \sum_{t=1}^{T} x_t \varepsilon_t$$

$$\mathbf{B_T} = F(y_\ell)'y_\ell - F(y_\ell)'X(X'X)^{-1}X'y_\ell$$
$$= \sum_{t=1}^{T} F(y_{t-1})y_{t-1} - \sum_{t=1}^{T} F(y_{t-1})x_t' \left(\sum_{t=1}^{T} x_t x_t' \right)^{-1} \sum_{t=1}^{T} x_t y_{t-1}$$

and the variance of A_T is given by $\sigma^2 EC_T$, where

$$\mathbf{C_T} = F(y_\ell)'F(y_\ell) - F(y_\ell)'X(X'X)^{-1}X'F(y_\ell)$$
$$= \sum_{t=1}^{T} F(y_{t-1})^2 - \sum_{t=1}^{T} F(y_{t-1})x_t' \left(\sum_{t=1}^{T} x_t x_t' \right)^{-1} \sum_{t=1}^{T} x_t F(y_{t-1})$$

For differenced lagged variables, themselves are used as the instruments without IGF transformation, details are explained in Chang(2002). The half-life calculated from the value of (1) assumes that shocks to the data decay monotonically, which is inappropriate for ADF regressions represented by (3), since in general shocks to an AR(p) will not decay at a constant rate. Murray and Papell (2002) calculate the half-life from the impulse response function of an AR(p) below,

$$y_t = c + \sum_{k=1}^{p} \phi_k y_{t-k} + \varepsilon_t \tag{4}$$

From the IGF estimates of (3), coefficients of (4) can be recalculated as follows:

$$\phi_1 = \alpha + \delta_1, \phi_2 = -(\delta_1 - \delta_2), \phi_3 = -(\delta_2 - \delta_3) \dots, \text{ and } \phi_p = -\delta_{p-1}. \tag{5}$$

When the coefficients are obtained, the k-period impulse response function (*irf* thereafter) for univariate AR(p) regression can be calculated. For convenience, we name (4) by ADF-AR(p).

(5) is widely used, for example, Murray and Papell (2002), however, not only is it subject to strict restriction, but also bias if some of right-hand-side variables of (4) are co-integrated. Therefore, instead of using (3) and (5) to indirectly calculate the coefficients of (4), we propose a Fully-Modified AR (p) to estimate (4) directly, the model is derived from Fully-Modified VAR of Phillips (1995). Section below continues the study.

2.3 Unrestricted fully-modified AR(p)

Phillips' (1995) FM-VAR is a level system regression with/without error correction terms (differenced terms). FM-VAR of Phillips (1995) generalized the asymptotics of Phillips and Hansen (1990), allowing full rank I(1) regressors and possible cointegration existed among lagged dependent variables. Mostly important, the asymptotics of FM-VAR is normal, or mixed normal, which allows us to construct confidence intervals and half life. The methodology for FM-AR(p) is illustrated below.

$$y_t = a + \alpha_1 y_{t-1} + \cdots \alpha_p y_{t-p} + u_{0t} = a + Ay_{t-} + u_{0t} \tag{6}$$

where A is an $1\times p$ coefficient vector and y_{t-} is a $p(p=p_1+p_2)$-dimensional vector of lagged y_t which are partitioned below:

$$H_1' y_{t-} = y_{1,t-} = u_{1t} \qquad p_1\times 1$$

$$H_2' \Delta y_{t-} = \Delta y_{2,t-} = u_{2t} \qquad p_2\times 1$$

Here $H=[H_1, H_2]$ is $p\times p$ orthogonal matrix and rotates the regressor space in (6) so that the model has the alternative form

$$y_t = A_1 y_{1,t-} + A_2 y_{2,t-} + u_{0t} \tag{7}$$

Here $A_1=AH_1$ and $A_2=AH_2$. The form of (7) usefully separates out the I(0) and I(1) components of the regressors in (6). However, the direction (H_1) in which the regressors are stationary will not be generally known in advance, not even will the rank of the cointegrating space of the regressors. Phillips' (1995) fully-modified correction has two steps:

The first step is to correct for the serial correlation to the LS estimator $\hat{A} = \left(y_{t-}' y_{t-}\right)^{-1} y_{t-}' y_t$ of (7). The endogeneity correction is achieved by modifying the dependent variable y_t in (7) with the transformation

$$y_t^+ = y_t - \hat{\Omega}_{0y_{t-}} \hat{\Omega}_{y_{t-}y_{t-}}^{-1} \Delta y_{t-} \tag{8}$$

In (8), $\hat{\Omega}$ denotes the kernel estimate of the long-run (lr) covariances of the variables denoted by the subscript:

$$\hat{\Omega}_{0y_{t-}} = lr\,\mathrm{cov}(u_{0t}, \Delta y_{t-}) \text{ and } \hat{\Omega}_{y_{t-}y_{t-}} = lr\,\mathrm{cov}(\Delta y_{t-}, \Delta y_{t-}) . \tag{8}$$

leads us to estimate the equation below

$$y_t - \hat{\Omega}_{0y_{t-}} \hat{\Omega}^{-1}_{y_{t-}y_{t-}} \Delta y_{t-} = A y_{t-} + u_{0t} - \Omega_{02}\Omega^{-1}_{22} u_{2t}$$

Phillips (1995, Pp. 1033-1034) shown that this transformation reduces to the ideal correction *asymptotically*, at least as far as the nonstationary components $y_{2,t-}$ are concerned. The stationary components $y_{1,t-}$ are present in differenced or I(-1) form in this transformation and have no effects asymptotically. Therefore, we can achieve an endogeneity correction with knowing the actual directions in which it is required or even the number of nonstationary regressors that need to be dealt with.
Secondly, the serial correction term has the form

$$\hat{\Delta}^{+}_{0y_{t-}} = \hat{\Delta}_{0y_{t-}} - \hat{\Omega}_{0y_{t-}} \hat{\Omega}^{-1}_{y_{t-}y_{t-}} \hat{\Delta}_{y_{t-}y_{t-}}$$

where $\hat{\Delta}_{0y_{t-}}$ and $\hat{\Delta}_{y_{t-}y_{t-}}$ denote the kernel estimates of the one-sided long-run covariances $\hat{\Delta}_{0y_{t-}} = lr\,\mathrm{cov}_{+}(u_{0t}, \Delta y_{t-})$ and $\hat{\Delta}_{y_{t-}y_{t-}} = lr\,\mathrm{cov}_{+}(\Delta y_{t-}, \Delta y_{t-})$.

Combining the endoneneity and serial corrections we have the FM formula for the parameter estimates

$$\hat{A}^{+} = \left(y'_{t-} y_{t-}\right)^{-1} \left(y'_{t-} y_t^{+} - T\hat{\Delta}^{+}_{0y_{t-}}\right) \tag{9}$$

For (9), the limit theory of FM estimates of the stationary components of the regressors is equivalent to that of LS, while the FM estimates of the nonstationary components retain their optimality properties as derived in Phillips and Hansen (1990); that is, they are asymptotically equivalent to the MLE estimates of the co-integrating matrix.
For the finite sample property of FM-AR, Appendix offers a simulation study illustrating a good performance of this estimator in calculating half-life of near I(1) process.

3. Empirical results

To illustrate these approaches, BIS real effective exchange rates (REER thereafter) of four economies (Germany, Japan, UK, and USA) are used, samples range from 1994M1 to 2010M12. BIS' REER is CPI-based and is a broad index of monthly averages, with 2005=100. Figure 1 plots the time series plot of them, with a horizontal line of the base year index. The Y-axis also illustrates the histogram to depict the distribution property of these data. The common feature of them is an apparent behavior of stochastic trend.
In Table 1, the upper panel DF-AR(1) presents the results of (1); the lower panel ADF-AR(p) summarizes those of (5), and the BIC criterion returns unanimously 2 lags. Comparing both results, taking Germany as an example, expressed in years, its half life takes 12.55 for DF-AR(1) and substantially drops to 0.916 for ADF-AR(2); similar finding is also found in Japan. UK and USA does not have finite bounds. Apparently, the dynamic lag structure is substantial.
Table 2 of FM-AR(2) tabulates more results. Unrestricted FM-AR(2) yields finite bounds of half-lives for all four economies, most of them are roughly less than two years. To be more informative, Figure 2 graphs the impulse response plot of Germany, expressed in month; clearly, the impulse response function of Germany has a rather wide confidence interval.

	GERMANY	JAPAN	UK	USA
Mean	101.40	108.02	95.97	99.52
Median	100.91	106.55	99.93	98.83
Maximum	116.79	151.11	107.81	116.00
Minimum	90.91	79.68	75.88	86.53
Std. Dev.	5.50	14.98	8.91	7.93
Skewness	0.63	0.42	-0.68	0.31
Kurtosis	3.09	2.99	2.04	2.10
JB(Prob.)	13.71(0.001)	6.073(0.048)	23.72(0.000)	10.18(0.006)

For each currency, there are 204 observations. JB(Prob.) is the Jarque-Bera statistic for normality with probability value in the parenthesis.

Table 1. Summary statistic

DF-AR(1)	α	Std	mean HL	HL, 90% CI	
				H_L	H_U
Germany	0.995	0.028	12.55	0.95	∞
Japan	0.984	0.028	3.58	0.78	∞
UK	1.025	0.014	∞	15.59	∞
USA	1.014	0.014	∞	4.29	∞
ADF-AR(2)	$\alpha+\delta_1$	$\delta_2-\delta_1$	mean HL	HL, 90% CI	
				H_L	H_U
Germany	1.180	-0.253	0.916	0.541	∞
Japan	1.272	-0.330	1.132	0.624	∞
UK	1.162	-0.159	∞	∞	∞
USA	1.332	-0.340	∞	1.911	∞

Note. HL =half-lives. BIC suggests two lags for four economies.

Table 2. IGF estimation results, in years, 1994M1-2010M12.

	α_1	α_2	mean HL	HL, 90% CI	
				H_L	H_U
Germany	1.121	-0.156	1.789	0.376	∞
Japan	1.292	-0.335	1.525	0.356	∞
UK	1.158	-0.191	1.926	0.258	∞
USA	1.270	-0.298	2.253	0.406	∞

Table 3. FM-AR(2) estimation results, in years, 1994M1-2010M12.

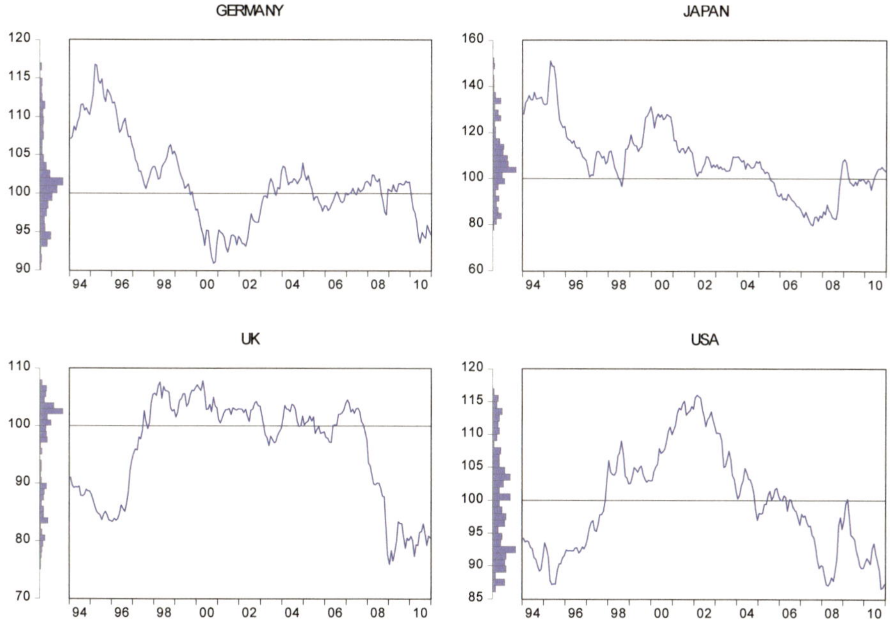

Fig. 1. Time series plot of four currencies' REER

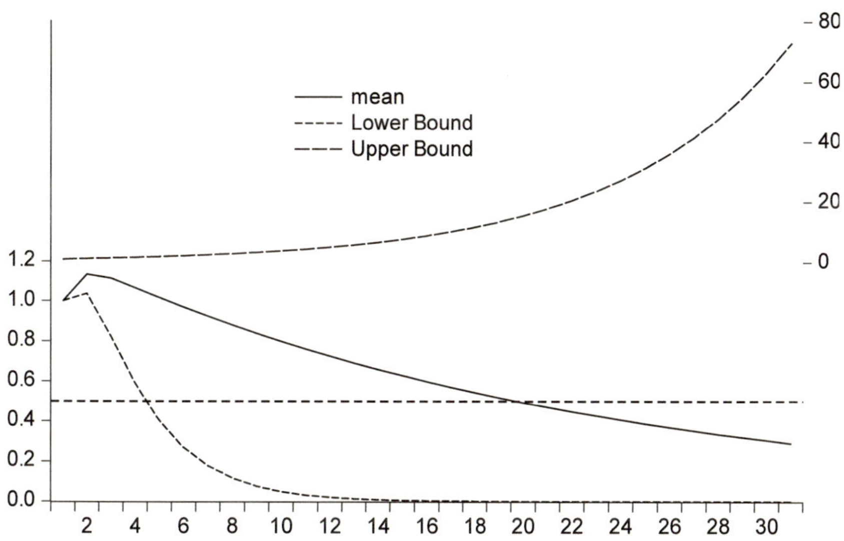

Fig. 2. Impulse-response plot of Germany, FM-AR(2), in month.

4. Conclusion

The empirical study of time series persistence uses two main approaches: unit root tests and half-life. However, reliance on unit root tests does NOT provide a measure of uncertainty of the estimates of finiteness or permanence of innovations because a rejection of the unit root null could still be consistent with a stationary process with highly persistent shocks. Because of near-unit root bias and resulting the lack of distribution, the empirical studies generally apply Andrews' (1993) median unbiasedness method to estimate the AR(1) coefficient to investigate the persistence behavior.

For AR(1) case, this paper contributes to the literature by applying the IGF approach of Phillips *et al.* (2004) to estimate the coefficients of near unit root process, IGF estimator is proved to be normal asymptotically, hence it is very easy to construct confidence intervals. For AR(p) case, moreover, instead of recalculation, we propose a unrestricted FM-AR(p) model, a slight extension of Phillips' (1995) FM-VAR, to estimate coefficients directly.

Our empirical illustration of real effective exchange rate indicates that FM-AR(p) is a useful and easy-to-use method to examine the econometric persistence.

5. Appendix: The finite sample properties of FM-AR

This paper shows that a FM estimator can ameliorate the small sample biases that arise from near unit root bias. Our attention here is focused on the class of dynamic AR(p). A Monte Carlo simulation is used here to investigate the performance, our results indicate that FM estimator successfully reduces the small-sample bias.

Assuming $\{y_t\}_{t=0}^{\infty}$ is governed by a AR(3) time series process generated from $(\mu, \sigma^2) = (0, 1)$, which satisfies the data-generating process specified below:

$$y_t = \alpha + \beta_1 y_{t-1} + \beta_2 y_{t-2} + \beta_3 y_{t-3} + \varepsilon_t \tag{1}$$

where ε_t ~*i.i.d.*. α and β's represent the associated parameters, and σ is the standard deviation. In our simulation, we generate an AR(3) process. The summation of the three coefficients measures the degree of persistence, the vector is parameterized below

Degree of Persistence 1: $\{\beta_1, \beta_2, \beta_3\} = \{0.90, 0.085, 0.015\}$,

Degree of Persistence 2: $\{\beta_1, \beta_2, \beta_3\} = \{0.90, 0.050, 0.015\}$

Degree of Persistence 3: $\{\beta_1, \beta_2, \beta_3\} = \{0.85, 0.050, 0.015\}$

and

$T \in \{200, 400, 800, 1500, 3000\}$

where T represents the vector of sampling size that are used in practice. The DGPs are characterized by a modest change in the innovation variance but allow for drastic changes in others.

Table A1 reports the characteristics of the finite-sample distribution of both estimators of the elements of estimates. These include the deviation of the estimate from the true parameter value, or bias, as well as measures of skewness and kurtosis. I compare the bias and normality to illustrate the problem. There are several main results.

Firstly, the biases are decreasing function of sample sizes. Even in small samples around 200 and 400, the biases are in the range of 10^{-2}. The bias for FM-AR is quite small.

Secondly, the variance bias exhibits the similar conclusion. AR(3) is generated from (0,1), the empirical bias is in the range of 10^{-3}, and is a decreasing function of sample size.

Finally, the normality property of distribution is drawn from skewness and kurtosis. Unfortunately, no regular pattern is found among three parameter estimates and is related to the persistence of parameter vector designed; in general, skewness is close to zero which gives normality an acceptable condition, although the excess kurtosis (>3) is found.

As a result, FM-AR is a feasible estimator to directly estimate AR(p), whose empirical applications also calls for further studies in the future.

{DGP coefficients} T	Estimates biases β_1	β_2	β_3	Skewness β_1	β_2	β_3	Kurtosis β_1	β_2	β_3	Variance biases $\sigma^2=1$
{0.9, 0.085, 0.015}										
200	-0.027	-0.036	0.007	0.194	-0.099	-0.301	5.48	2.88	0.451	-0.029
400	-0.023	-0.030	0.011	0.186	-0.174	-0.320	5.27	3.25	4.502	-0.024
800	-0.020	-0.027	0.015	0.122	-0.25	-0.314	5.45	3.88	4.923	-0.018
1500	-0.019	-0.024	0.018	0.117	-0.337	-0.365	5.79	4.56	5.328	-0.014
3000	-0.019	-0.023	0.021	0.108	-0.399	-0.445	6.27	5.36	5.847	-0.011
{0.9, 0.05, 0.015}										
200	-0.020	-0.024	-0.016	0.060	-0.19	-0.058	5.10	3.12	4.25	-0.029
400	-0.020	-0.017	-0.014	0.030	-0.27	-0.027	5.50	3.45	4.73	-0.019
800	-0.017	-0.015	-0.014	-0.009	-0.336	-0.0005	5.63	4.06	5.01	-0.012
1500	-0.016	-0.014	-0.013	-0.038	-0.376	-0.025	5.94	4.80	5.40	-0.0073
3000	-0.015	-0.013	-0.012	-0.049	-0.432	-0.057	6.49	5.67	5.92	-0.0042
{0.85, 0.05, 0.015}										
200	-0.020	-0.0067	-0.040	0.340	-0.17	-0.09	5.6	3.04	4.74	-0.02
400	-0.016	-0.0079	-0.038	0.190	-0.15	-0.124	5.4	3.29	4.72	-0.015
800	-0.013	-0.0076	-0.038	0.110	-0.16	-0.12	5.4	3.76	5.12	-0.009
1500	-0.011	-0.0060	-0.038	0.077	-0.198	-0.108	5.6	4.36	5.54	-0.0045
3000	-0.010	-0.0058	-0.038	0.056	-0.233	-0.111	6.1	5.10	6.08	-0.0015

Table A1. Biases and skewness of the empirical distribution

6. References

Andrews, D. (1993) Exactly median-unbiased estimation of first-order autoregressive/ unit root models. *Econometrica* 61, 139- 165.

Cerrato Mario , Neil Kellard, Nicholas Sarantis (2008) the purchasing power parity persistence puzzle: evidence from black market exchange rates. *Manchester School,* 76(4), 405–423.

Chang, Y. (2002) Nonlinear IV unit root tests in panels with cross-sectional dependency. *Journal of Econometrics* 110, 261-292.

DeJong, D.N., J.C. Nankervis, N.E. Savin and C.H.Whiteman, (1992) Integration versus trend stationarity in time series. *Econometrica* 60, 423-433.

Dickey, D.A., Fuller, W.A. (1979) Distribution of the estimators for autoregressive time series with a unit root. *Journal of American Statistical Association* 74, 427–431.

Murray C. J., Papell D. H. (2002) The purchasing power parity persistence paradigm. *Journal of International Economics* 56, 1-19.

Orcutt, G.H. (1948) A study of the autoregressive nature of the time series used for Tinbergen's model of the economic system of the United States 1919–1932, *Journal of the Royal Statistical Society* 10 (1948), pp. 1–53 Seires B.

Papell, David H. (1997) Searching for stationarity: purchasing power parity under the current float. *Journal of International Economics*, 43, 313–323.
Phillips P. C. B., B.E. Hansen (1990) Statistical inference in instrumental variables with I(1) regressors. *Review of Economic Studies*, 57(2), 99-125.
Phillips P. C. B., Park, J. Y., Chang Y.(2004) Nonlinear instrument variable estimation of an autoregression. *Journal of Econometrics* 118, 219-246.
Phillips P. C. B. (1995) Fully-modified least squares and vector autoregression. *Econometrica*, 63(5), 1023-1078.
So, B.S., Shin, D.W. (1999) Recursive mean adjustment in time-series inferences. *Statistics & Probability Letters* 43, 65–73.

3

Recent Developments in Seasonal Volatility Models

Julieta Frank[1], Melody Ghahramani[2] and A. Thavaneswaran[1]
[1]*University of Manitoba*
[2]*University of Winnipeg*
Canada

1. Introduction

It is well-known that many financial time series such as stock returns exhibit leptokurtosis and time-varying volatility (Bollerslev, 1986; Engle, 1982; Nicholls & Quinn, 1982). The generalized autoregressive conditional heteroscedasticity (GARCH) and the random coefficient autoregressive (RCA) models have been extensively used to capture the time-varying behavior of the volatility. Studies using GARCH models commonly assume that the time series is conditionally normally distributed; however, the kurtosis implied by the normal GARCH tends to be lower than the sample kurtosis observed in many time series (Bollerslev, 1986). Thavaneswaran et al. (2005a) use an ARMA representation to derive the kurtosis of various classes of GARCH models such as power GARCH, non-Gaussian GARCH, non-stationary and random coefficient GARCH. Recently, Thavaneswaran et al. (2009) have extended the results to stationary RCA processes with GARCH errors and Paseka et al. (2010) further extended the results to RCA processes with stochastic volatility (SV) errors.

Seasonal behavior is commonly observed in financial time series, as well as in currency and commodity markets. The opening and closure of the markets, time-of-the-day and day-of-the-week effects, weekends and vacation periods cause changes in the trading volume that translates into regular changes in price variability. Financial, currency, and commodity data also respond to new information entering into the market, which usually follow seasonal patterns (Frank & Garcia, 2009). Recently there has been growing interest in using seasonal volatility models, for example Bollerslev (1996), Baillie & Bollerslev (1990) and Franses & Paap (2000). Doshi et al. (2011) discuss the kurtosis and volatility forecasts for seasonal GARCH models. Ghysels & Osborn (2001) review studies performed on seasonal volatility behavior in several markets. Most of the studies use GARCH models with dummy variables in the volatility equation, and a few of them have been extended to a more flexible form such as the periodic GARCH. However, even though much research has been performed on volatility models applied to market data such as stock returns, more general specifications accounting for seasonal volatility have been little explored.

First, we derive the kurtosis of a simple time series model with seasonal behavior in the mean. Then we introduce various classes of seasonal volatility models and study the moments, forecast error variance, and discuss applications in option pricing. We extend the results for non-seasonal volatility models to seasonal volatility models. For the seasonal GARCH model, we follow the results obtained by Doshi et al. (2011) and extend it to the RCA-seasonal GARCH model. The multiplicative seasonal GARCH model is appropriate for time series where significant autocorrelation exists at seasonal and at adjacent non-seasonal lags. We also propose and derive the expressions for the kurtosis of seasonal SV models and other models such as the RCA with seasonal SV errors.

We also derive the closed-form expression for the variance of the l-steps ahead forecast error in terms of (ψ, Ψ) weights, model parameters and the kurtosis of the error distribution. We show that the kurtosis for the non-seasonal model turns out to be a special case. Option pricing with seasonal GARCH volatility is also discussed in some detail. The moments derived for the seasonal volatility models and the l-steps ahead forecast error variance provide more accurate estimates of market data behavior and help investors, decision makers, and other market participants develop improved trading strategies.

2. Seasonal AR models with GARCH errors

We first start with a seasonal AR(1) model with simple GARCH errors of the form,

$$y_t - \mu = \beta(y_{t-s} - \mu) + \epsilon_{t-1}^2 \epsilon_t \tag{1}$$

where s represents the seasonal period and ϵ_t is a sequence of independent random variables. The following lemma, given in Ghahramani & Thavaneswaran (2007), can be used to derive the second and fourth moments of the process in (1).

Lemma 2.1. For a stationary process and finite eighth moment, the expected value and kurtosis $K^{(y)}$ of the process (1) is given by:

(a)

$$E(y_t - \mu)^2 = \frac{E(\epsilon_{t-1}^4)E(\epsilon_t^2)}{1-\beta^2},$$

(b)

$$K^{(y)} = \frac{E[(y_t-\mu)^4]}{Var(y_t)^2} = \frac{6\beta^2[E(\epsilon_{t-1}^4)E(\epsilon_t^2)]^2 + E(\epsilon_{t-1}^8)E(\epsilon_t^4)(1-\beta^2)}{(1+\beta^2)(E(\epsilon_{t-1}^4)E(\epsilon_t^2))^2},$$

(c) if ϵ_t are assumed to be i.i.d. N(0,σ_ϵ^2), then E$[\epsilon_t^{2n}] = ((2n)!/2^n(n!))\sigma_\epsilon^{2n}$ and hence

$$K^{(y)} = \left[\frac{35-29\beta^2}{(1+\beta^2)}\right].$$

3. AR Models with seasonal GARCH errors

AR models are the most common representation used in time series analysis. Multiplicative seasonal GARCH errors of the form GARCH(p,q)x$(P,Q)_s$ have been suggested by Doshi et al. (2011). Consider the following model,

$$y_t = \beta y_{t-1} + \epsilon_t \tag{2}$$

$$\epsilon_t = \sqrt{h_t} Z_t \tag{3}$$

$$\theta(B)\Theta(L)h_t = \omega + \alpha(B)\epsilon_t^2 \tag{4}$$

where $\{Z_t\}$ is a sequence of independent and identically distributed (i.i.d.) random variables with zero mean and unit variance, $\alpha(B) = \theta(B)\Theta(L) - \phi(B)\Phi(L)$, $\phi(B) = 1 - \sum_{i=1}^{p} \phi_i B^i$,

$\theta(B) = 1 - \sum_{i=1}^{q} \theta_i B^i$, $\Phi(L) = 1 - \sum_{i=1}^{P} \Phi_i L^i$, $\Theta(L) = 1 - \sum_{i=1}^{Q} \Theta_i L^i$, $L = B^s$, and all coefficients are assumed to be positive.

Letting $u_t = \epsilon_t^2 - h_t$ and $\sigma_u^2 = \text{var}(u_t)$, (4) may be written as,

$$\phi_p(B)\Phi_P(L)\epsilon_t^2 = \omega + \theta_q(B)\Theta_Q(L)u_t, \tag{5}$$

which has a seasonal ARMA(p,q)x$(P,Q)_s$ representation for ϵ_t^2. Note that when $P = Q = 0$, (5) simplifies to an ARMA(max$\{p,q\}$,q) representation for ϵ_t^2, corresponding to the general GARCH(p,q) model.

We assume that $|\beta| < 1$; thus, y_t as given in (2) is stationary. The moving average representation is $y_t = \sum_{j=0}^{\infty} \psi_j \epsilon_{t-j}$ where $\{\psi_j\}$ is a sequence of constants and $\sum_{j=0}^{\infty} \psi_j^2 < \infty$. The ψ_j's are obtained from $(1 - \beta B)\psi(B) = 1$ where $\psi(B) = 1 + \sum_{j=1}^{\infty} \psi_j B^j$.

We also assume that all the zeros of the polynomial $\phi(B)\Phi(L)$ lie outside the unit circle; thus, ϵ_t^2 as given in (5) is stationary. The moving average representation is $\epsilon_t^2 = \mu + \sum_{j=0}^{\infty} \Psi_j u_{t-j}$ where $\{\Psi_j\}$ is a sequence of constants and $\sum_{j=0}^{\infty} \Psi_j^2 < \infty$. The Ψ_j's are obtained from $\Psi(B)\phi(B)\Phi(L) = \theta(B)\Theta(L)$ where $\Psi(B) = 1 + \sum_{j=1}^{\infty} \Psi_j B^j$.

Next, we provide the kurtosis, the forecast, and the forecast error variance for an AR(1)-seasonal GARCH(p,q)x$(P,Q)_s$.

Lemma 3.1. For the stationary AR(1) process y_t with multiplicative seasonal GARCH innovations as in (2)– (4) we have the following relationships:

$$\text{(i)} \quad E(y_t^2) = \frac{E(\epsilon_t^2)}{1-\beta^2}, \tag{6}$$

$$\text{(ii)} \quad E(y_t^4) = \frac{6\beta^2[E(\epsilon_t^2)]^2 + (1-\beta^2)E(\epsilon_t^4)}{(1-\beta^2)(1-\beta^4)}, \tag{7}$$

$$\text{(iii)} \quad K^{(y)} = \frac{E(y_t^4)}{[E(y_t^2)]^2} = \frac{6\beta^2(1-\beta^2)}{1-\beta^4} + \frac{(1-\beta^2)^2}{1-\beta^4}K^{(\epsilon)}. \tag{8}$$

The kurtosis for ϵ_t, $K^{(\epsilon)}$, is given below.

Lemma 3.2. For the stationary process (3) with finite fourth moment, the kurtosis $K^{(\epsilon)}$ is given by:

(a) $$K^{(\epsilon)} = \frac{E(Z_t^4)}{E(Z_t^4) - [E(Z_t^4) - 1]\sum_{j=0}^{\infty} \Psi_j^2}.$$

(b) The variance of the ϵ_t^2 process is given by $\gamma_0^{\epsilon^2} = \sum_{j=0}^{\infty} \Psi_j^2 \sigma_u^2$

where $\sigma_u^2 = \dfrac{\mu^2(K^{(\epsilon)} - 1)}{\sum_{j=0}^{\infty} \Psi_j^2}$ and $\mu = E(\epsilon_t^2) = \dfrac{\omega}{\left(1 - \sum_{i=1}^{p} \phi_i\right)\left(1 - \sum_{i=1}^{P} \Phi_i\right)}$.

Part (a) is derived in Thavaneswaran et al. (2005a) where examples are given with Ψ-weights derived for non-seasonal GARCH models. The Ψ-weights for examples of seasonal GARCH models, and the proof of part (b), are given in Doshi et al. (2011).

Extending Doshi et al. (2011), we derive the $K^{(y)}$ for AR(1)-seasonal GARCH(p,q)x$(P,Q)_s$ models as follows.

Example 3.1. For a stationary autoregressive process of order one, AR(1), with multiplicative seasonal GARCH $(0,1)$x$(0,1)_s$ errors of the form:

$$
\begin{aligned}
y_t &= \beta y_{t-1} + \epsilon_t \\
\epsilon_t &= \sqrt{h_t} Z_t \\
\epsilon_t^2 &= \omega + (1-\theta B)(1-\Theta L) u_t
\end{aligned}
$$

where $u_t = \epsilon_t^2 - h_t$, θ is the moving average parameter and Θ is the seasonal moving average parameter. The Ψ-weights are given in Doshi et al. (2011) as $\Psi_1 = -\theta_1$, $\Psi_s = -\Theta$, $\Psi_{s+1} = \theta\Theta$, and $\Psi_j = 0$ otherwise. It can be shown that $\sum_{j=0}^{\infty} \Psi_j^2 = (1+\theta^2)(1+\Theta^2)$. Then, the kurtosis of y_t is:

$$
K^{(y)} = \frac{6\beta^2(1-\beta^2)}{(1-\beta^4)} + \frac{(1-\beta^2)^2}{(1-\beta^4)} \frac{E(Z_t^4)}{E(Z_t^4) - [E(Z_t^4)-1](1+\theta^2)(1+\Theta^2)}, \tag{9}
$$

which for a conditionally normally distributed Z_t reduces to:

$$
K^{(y)} = \frac{6\beta^2(1-\beta^2)}{(1-\beta^4)} + \frac{(1-\beta^2)^2}{(1-\beta^4)} \frac{3}{[3-2(1+\theta^2)(1+\Theta^2)]}.
$$

Example 3.2. For a stationary autoregressive process of order one, AR(1), with multiplicative seasonal GARCH $(0,1)$x$(1,0)_s$ errors of the form,

$$
\begin{aligned}
y_t &= \beta y_{t-1} + \epsilon_t \\
\epsilon_t &= \sqrt{h_t} Z_t \\
(1-\Phi L)\epsilon_t^2 &= \omega + (1-\theta B) u_t
\end{aligned}
$$

where Φ is the seasonal autoregressive parameter and θ is the moving average parameter. The Ψ-weights given in Doshi et al. (2011) are as follows: $\Psi_1 = -\theta$, $\Psi_s = -\Phi$, $\Psi_{s+1} = -\theta\Phi$, $\Psi_{2s} = \Phi^2, \ldots, \Psi_{ks} = \Phi^k, \Psi_{ks+1} = -\theta\Phi^k$, where $k = 1, 2, \ldots$ It can be shown that $\sum_{j=0}^{\infty} \Psi_j^2 = (1+\theta^2)/(1-\Theta^2)$. Then, the kurtosis of y_t is:

$$
K^{(y)} = \frac{6\beta^2(1-\beta^2)}{(1-\beta^4)} + \frac{(1-\beta^2)^2}{(1-\beta^4)} \frac{E(Z_t^4)}{E(Z_t^4) - [E(Z_t^4)-1]\left(\frac{1+\theta^2}{1-\Phi^2}\right)},
$$

which for a conditionally normally distributed Z_t reduces to:

$$
K^{(y)} = \frac{6\beta^2(1-\beta^2)}{(1-\beta^4)} + \frac{(1-\beta^2)^2}{(1-\beta^4)} \frac{3(1-\Phi^2)}{(1-3\Phi^2-2\theta^2)}.
$$

Example 3.3. For a stationary autoregressive process of order one, AR(1), with multiplicative seasonal GARCH $(1,0)\text{x}(1,0)_s$ errors of the form,

$$\begin{aligned} y_t &= \beta y_{t-1} + \epsilon_t \\ \epsilon_t &= \sqrt{h_t} Z_t \\ (1-\phi B)(1-\Phi L)\epsilon_t^2 &= \omega + u_t \end{aligned}$$

where ϕ is the autoregressive parameter and Φ is the seasonal autoregressive parameter. The Ψ-weights given in Doshi et al. (2011) are as follows: $\Psi_1 = \phi, \Psi_2 = \phi^2, \ldots, \Psi_{s-1} = \phi^{s-1}, \Psi_s = \phi^2 + \Phi, \ldots, \Psi_j = \phi\Psi_{j-1} + \Phi\Psi_{j-s} - \phi\Phi\Psi_{j-s}$. It can be shown that $\sum_{j=0}^{\infty} \Psi_j^2 = \dfrac{1+2\phi^s\Phi^2+\Phi^2}{1-\phi^2}$. Then, the kurtosis of y_t is:

$$K^{(y)} = \frac{6\beta^2(1-\beta^2)}{(1-\beta^4)} + \frac{(1-\beta^2)^2}{(1-\beta^4)} \frac{E(Z_t^4)}{E(Z_t^4) - [E(Z_t^4)-1]\left(\dfrac{1+2\phi^s\Phi+\Phi^2}{1-\phi^2}\right)},$$

which for a conditionally normally distributed Z_t reduces to:

$$K^{(y)} = \frac{6\beta^2(1-\beta^2)}{(1-\beta^4)} + \frac{(1-\beta^2)^2}{(1-\beta^4)} \frac{3(1-\phi^2)}{(1-3\phi^2-4\phi^s\Phi-2\Phi^2)}.$$

Forecast error variance

Thavaneswaran et al. (2005a) derive the expression for the forecast error variance of various classes of zero mean GARCH(p,q) processes, in terms of the kurtosis and Ψ-weights. Thavaneswaran & Ghahramani (2008) extend the results for ARMA (p,q) processes with GARCH (P,Q) errors. In this section we extend the results to AR models with multiplicative seasonal GARCH$(p,q)\text{x}(P,Q)_s$ errors.

Theorem 3.1. Let $y_n(l)$ be the l-steps-ahead minimum mean square forecast of y_{n+l} and let $e_n^{(y)}(l) = y_{n+l} - y_n(l)$ be the corresponding forecast error. The variance of the l-steps-ahead forecast error of y_{n+l} for the AR(1) model with seasonal GARCH errors as given in (2)- (4) is:

$$\text{Var}[e_n^{(y)}(l)] = \frac{\omega}{\left(1-\sum_{i=1}^{p}\phi_i\right)\left(1-\sum_{i=1}^{P}\Phi_i\right)} \sum_{j=0}^{l-1} \psi_j^2. \tag{10}$$

Proof. The theorem follows from the fact that for a stationary process with uncorrelated error noise ϵ_t the variance of the l-steps ahead forecast error is $\sigma_\epsilon^2 \sum_{j=0}^{l-1} \psi_j^2$ and from part (b) of Lemma 3.2.

We now have expressions for the variance of the l-steps-ahead forecast error of y_{n+l} for the previously discussed AR(1)-GARCH$(p,q)\text{x}(P,Q)_s$ models:

AR(1)-GARCH$(0,1)\text{x}(0,1)_s$ $\qquad$ $\text{Var}[e_n^{(y)}(l)] = \omega \sum_{j=0}^{l-1} \beta^{2j}$

AR(1)-GARCH$(0,1)$x$(1,0)_s$ $\quad$ $\text{Var}[e_n^{(y)}(l)] = \frac{\omega}{1-\Phi}\sum_{j=0}^{l-1}\beta^{2j}$

AR(1)-GARCH$(1,0)$x$(1,0)_s$ $\quad$ $\text{Var}[e_n^{(y)}(l)] = \frac{\omega}{(1-\phi)(1-\Phi)}\sum_{j=0}^{l-1}\beta^{2j}.$

In the literature on time series analysis, the error variance is estimated by the residual sum of squares. If we denote the squared residual as $Y_t = (y_t - \hat{\beta}y_{t-1})^2$, then we can forecast the conditional variance, $\text{var}(y_t|y_{t-1},\ldots) = h_t$, by using $Y_1,\ldots,Y_{t-1}$.

Theorem 3.2. Let $Y_n(l)$ be the l-steps-ahead minimum mean square forecast of Y_{n+l} and let $e_n^{(Y)}(l) = Y_{n+l} - Y_n(l)$ be the corresponding forecast error. The variance of the l-steps-ahead forecast error of Y_{n+l} is given by:

$$\text{Var}[e_n^{(Y)}(l)] = \sigma_u^2\sum_{j=0}^{l-1}\Psi_j^2 = \frac{\omega^2}{\left[\sum_{j=0}^{\infty}\Psi_j^2\right]\left[1-\sum_{i=1}^{p}\phi_i\right]^2\left[1-\sum_{i=1}^{P}\Phi_i\right]^2}[K^{(\epsilon)}-1]\left[\sum_{j=0}^{l-1}\Psi_j^2\right] \tag{11}$$

where, from (8), $K^{(\epsilon)} = \frac{1-\beta^4}{(1-\beta^2)^2}K^{(y)} - \frac{6\beta^2}{1-\beta^2}.$

Proof. The proof follows from part (b) of Lemma 3.2.

We now have expressions for the variance of the l-steps-ahead forecast error of Y_{n+l} for the previously discussed AR(1)-GARCH(p,q)x$(P,Q)_s$ models:

AR(1)-GARCH$(0,1)$x$(0,1)_s$ $\quad$ $\text{Var}[e_n^{(Y)}(l)] = \frac{(K^{(\epsilon)}-1)\mu^2}{(1+\theta^2)(1+\Theta^2)}\sum_{j=0}^{l-1}\Psi_j^2$

AR(1)-GARCH$(0,1)$x$(1,0)_s$ $\quad$ $\text{Var}[e_n^{(Y)}(l)] = \frac{(K^{(\epsilon)}-1)\mu^2(1-\Phi^2)}{1+\theta^2}\sum_{j=0}^{l-1}\Psi_j^2$

AR(1)-GARCH$(1,0)$x$(1,0)_s$ $\quad$ $\text{Var}[e_n^{(Y)}(l)] = \frac{(K^{(\epsilon)}-1)\mu^2(1-\phi^2)}{1+2\phi^s\Phi+\Phi^2}\sum_{j=0}^{l-1}\Psi_j^2$

which are similar to the expressions given in Doshi et al. (2011). Here, $K^{(\epsilon)}$ is given in Theorem 3.2. and expressions for $K^{(y)}$ are given in Examples 3.1, 3.2, and 3.3.

4. RCA models with seasonal GARCH errors

The random coefficient autoregressive (RCA) model as proposed by Nicholls & Quinn (1982) has the form,

$$y_t = (\beta + b_t)y_{t-1} + \epsilon_t \tag{12}$$

where $\begin{pmatrix} b_t \\ \epsilon_t \end{pmatrix} \sim N\left(\begin{pmatrix} 0 \\ 0 \end{pmatrix}, \begin{pmatrix} \sigma_b^2 & 0 \\ 0 & \sigma_\epsilon^2 \end{pmatrix}\right)$ and $\beta^2 + \sigma_b^2 < 1$.

Thavaneswaran et al. (2009) derive the moments for the RCA model with GARCH(p, q) errors. Here we propose the RCA model with seasonal GARCH innovations of the following form,

$$y_t = (\beta + b_t)y_{t-1} + \epsilon_t \tag{13}$$

$$\epsilon_t = \sqrt{h_t} Z_t \tag{14}$$

$$\theta(B)\Theta(L)h_t = \omega + \alpha(B)\epsilon_t^2 \tag{15}$$

where $Z_t, \theta(B), \Theta(L), \alpha(B)$ were defined in Section 2.
The general expression for the kurtosis $K^{(y)}$ parallels the one in Thavaneswaran et al. (2009) for non-seasonal GARCH innovations and can be written as follows.
Lemma 4.1. For the stationary RCA process y_t with GARCH innovations as in (13)– (15) we have the following relationships:

$$\text{(i)}\ \ E(y_t^2) = \frac{E(\epsilon_t^2)}{1 - (\beta^2 + \sigma_b^2)}, \tag{16}$$

$$\text{(ii)}\ \ E(y_t^4) = \frac{6(\beta^2 + \sigma_b^2)[E(\epsilon_t^2)]^2 + [1 - (\beta^2 + \sigma_b^2)]E(\epsilon_t^4)}{1 - (3\sigma_b^4 + \beta^4 + 6\beta^2\sigma_b^2)[1 - (\beta^2 + \sigma_b^2)]}, \tag{17}$$

$$\text{(iii)}\ \ K^{(y)} = \frac{6(\beta^2 + \sigma_b^2)[1 - (\beta^2 + \sigma_b^2)]}{1 - (3\sigma_b^4 + \beta^4 + 6\beta^2\sigma_b^2)} + \frac{[1 - (\beta^2 + \sigma_b^2)]^2}{1 - (3\sigma_b^4 + \beta^4 + 6\beta^2\sigma_b^2)} K^{(\epsilon)}. \tag{18}$$

If Z_t is normally distributed, then the above equations can be written as:

$$\text{(i)}\ \ E(y_t^2) = \frac{E(h_t)}{1 - (\beta^2 + \sigma_b^2)}, \tag{19}$$

$$\text{(ii)}\ \ E(y_t^4) = \frac{6(\beta^2 + \sigma_b^2)}{[1 - (\beta^2 + \sigma_b^2)](1 - 6\beta^2\sigma_b^2 - \beta^4 - 3\sigma_b^4)}[E(h_t)]^2 + \frac{3E(h_t^2)}{1 - 6\beta^2\sigma_b^2 - \beta^4 - 3\sigma_b^4}, \tag{20}$$

$$\text{(iii)}\ \ K^{(y)} = \frac{6(\beta^2 + \sigma_b^2)[1 - (\beta^2 + \sigma_b^2)]}{1 - 6\beta^2\sigma_b^2 - \beta^4 - 3\sigma_b^4} + \frac{3(1 - \beta^2 - \sigma_b^2)}{1 - 6\beta^2\sigma_b^2 - \beta^4 - 3\sigma_b^4} \frac{E(h_t^2)}{[E(h_t)]^2}. \tag{21}$$

Thavaneswaran et al. (2005a) show that:

$$\frac{E(h_t^2)}{[E(h_t)]^2} = \frac{1}{E(Z_t^4) - [E(Z_t^4) - 1]\sum_{j=0}^{\infty} \Psi_j^2},$$

which for a conditionally normally distributed ϵ_t reduces to $\dfrac{1}{3 - 2\sum_{j=0}^{\infty} \Psi_j^2}$.

Example 4.1. RCA(1) with multiplicative seasonal GARCH (0,1)x(0,1) process

$$y_t = (\beta + b_t)y_{t-1} + \epsilon_t$$

$$\epsilon_t = \sqrt{h_t} Z_t$$

$$\epsilon_t^2 = \omega + (1 - \theta B)(1 - \Theta L)u_t$$

where $u_t = \epsilon_t^2 - h_t$.The Ψ-weights are given in example 3.1. Then, the kurtosis of y_t for a conditionally normally distributed Z_t is:

$$K^{(y)} = \frac{6(\sigma_b^2 + \beta^2)(1 - \beta^2 - \sigma_b^2)}{1 - 6\beta^2\sigma_b^2 - \beta^4 - 3\sigma_b^4} + \frac{3(1 - \beta^2 - \sigma_b^2)}{(1 - 6\beta^2\sigma_b^2 - \beta^4 - 3\sigma_b^4)[3 - 2(1 + \theta^2)(1 + \Theta^2)]}.$$

Example 4.2. RCA(1) with multiplicative seasonal GARCH (0,1)x(1,0) process

$$\begin{aligned} y_t &= (\beta + b_t)y_{t-1} + \epsilon_t \\ \epsilon_t &= \sqrt{h_t} Z_t \\ (1 - \Phi L)\epsilon_t^2 &= \omega + (1 - \theta B)u_t \end{aligned}$$

The Ψ-weights are given in example 3.2. Then, the kurtosis of y_t for a conditionally normally distributed Z_t is:

$$K^{(y)} = \frac{6(\sigma_b^2 + \beta^2)(1 - \beta^2 - \sigma_b^2)}{1 - 6\beta^2\sigma_b^2 - \beta^4 - 3\sigma_b^4} + \frac{3(1 - \beta^2 - \sigma_b^2)}{(1 - 6\beta^2\sigma_b^2 - \beta^4 - 3\sigma_b^4)\left[3 - 2\left(\frac{1 + \theta^2}{1 - \Phi^2}\right)\right]}.$$

Example 4.3. RCA(1) with multiplicative seasonal GARCH (1,0)x(1,0) process

$$\begin{aligned} y_t &= (\beta + b_t)y_{t-1} + \epsilon_t \\ \epsilon_t &= \sqrt{h_t} Z_t \\ (1 - \phi B)(1 - \Phi L)\epsilon_t^2 &= \omega + u_t \end{aligned}$$

The Ψ-weights are given in example 3.3. Then, the kurtosis of y_t for a conditionally normally distributed Z_t is:

$$K^{(y)} = \frac{6(\sigma_b^2 + \beta^2)(1 - \beta^2 - \sigma_b^2)}{1 - 6\beta^2\sigma_b^2 - \beta^4 - 3\sigma_b^4} + \frac{3(1 - \beta^2 - \sigma_b^2)}{(1 - 6\beta^2\sigma_b^2 - \beta^4 - 3\sigma_b^4)\left[3 - 2\left(\frac{1 + 2\phi^s\Phi + \Phi^2}{1 - \Phi^2}\right)\right]}.$$

Forecast error variance

Thavaneswaran & Ghahramani (2008) derive the expression for the variance of the forecast error for a RCA(1) process with non-seasonal GARCH (1,1) errors. In this section we expand the results for the more general RCA(1) process with seasonal GARCH(p,q)x$(P,Q)_s$ errors.

Theorem 4.1. Let $y_n(l)$ be the l-steps-ahead minimum mean square forecast of y_{n+l} and let $e_n^{(y)}(l) = y_{n+l} - y_n(l)$ be the corresponding forecast error. The variance of the l-steps-ahead forecast error of y_{n+l} for the RCA(1) model with seasonal GARCH errors as given in (13)- (15) is:

$$\text{Var}[e_n^{(y)}(l)] = \frac{\omega(1 - \beta^2)}{\left(1 - \sum_{i=1}^{p}\phi_i\right)\left(1 - \sum_{i=1}^{P}\Phi_i\right)(1 - \beta^2 - \sigma_b^2)} \sum_{j=0}^{l-1}\beta^{2j}. \tag{22}$$

Proof. The y_t process is second order stationary with autocorrelation $\rho_k = \beta^k$ and variance $\sigma_\epsilon^2/(1 - \beta^2 - \sigma_b^2)$. Hence, y_t has a valid moving average representation of the form $y_t^* =$

$\sum_{j=0}^{\infty} \beta^j a_{t-j}$, where a_t is an uncorrelated sequence with variance σ_a^2. By equating the variance of y_t^* to the variance of y_t we have $\sigma_\epsilon^2/(1-\beta^2-\sigma_b^2) = \sigma_a^2/(1-\beta^2)$, and $\sigma_a^2 = \sigma_\epsilon^2(1-\beta^2)/(1-\beta^2-\sigma_b^2)$.

Note: When $\sigma_b^2 = 0$, $\text{var}[e_n^{(y)}(l)]$ in Theorem 4.1 reduces to $\text{var}[e_n^{(y)}(l)]$ in Theorem 3.1 for the AR model with seasonal GARCH errors.

We now have expressions for the variance of the l-steps-ahead forecast error of y_{n+l} for the previously discussed RCA(1)-GARCH(p,q)x$(P,Q)_s$ models:

RCA(1)-GARCH$(0,1)$x$(0,1)_s$ $\quad \text{Var}[e_n^{(y)}(l)] = \dfrac{\omega(1-\beta^2)}{(1-\beta^2-\sigma_b^2)} \sum_{j=0}^{l-1} \beta^{2j}$

RCA(1)-GARCH$(0,1)$x$(1,0)_s$ $\quad \text{Var}[e_n^{(y)}(l)] = \dfrac{\omega(1-\beta^2)}{(1-\Phi)(1-\beta^2-\sigma_b^2)} \sum_{j=0}^{l-1} \beta^{2j},$

RCA(1)-GARCH$(1,0)$x$(1,0)_s$ $\quad \text{Var}[e_n^{(y)}(l)] = \dfrac{\omega(1-\beta^2)}{(1-\phi)(1-\Phi)(1-\beta^2-\sigma_b^2)} \sum_{j=0}^{l-1} \beta^{2j}.$

Theorem 4.2. Let $Y_t = [y_t - (\hat{\beta} + b_t)y_{t-1}]^2$. Also, let $Y_n(l)$ be the l-steps-ahead minimum mean square forecast of Y_{n+l} and let $e_n^{(Y)}(l) = Y_{n+l} - Y_n(l)$ be the corresponding forecast error. The variance of the l-steps-ahead forecast error of Y_{n+l} for the RCA(1) model with seasonal GARCH errors as given in (13)- (15) is:

$$\text{Var}[e_n^{(Y)}(l)] = \sigma_u^2 \sum_{j=0}^{l-1} \Psi_j^2 = \frac{\omega^2}{\left[\sum_{j=0}^{\infty} \Psi_j^2\right] \left[1 - \sum_{i=1}^{p} \phi_i\right]^2 \left[1 - \sum_{i=1}^{P} \Phi_i\right]^2} [K^{(\epsilon)} - 1] \left[\sum_{j=0}^{l-1} \Psi_j^2\right] \qquad (23)$$

where, from (18), $K^{(\epsilon)} = \dfrac{1-(3\sigma_b^4 + \beta^4 + 6\beta^2\sigma_b^2)}{[1-(\beta^2+\sigma_b^2)]^2} K^{(y)} - \dfrac{6(\beta^2+\sigma_b^2)}{1-(\beta^2+\sigma_b^2)}.$

Proof. The proof follows from part (b) of Lemma 3.2.

Note: When $\sigma_b^2 = 0$, $K^{(\epsilon)}$ in Theorem 4.2 reduces to $K^{(\epsilon)}$ in Theorem 3.2 for the AR model with seasonal GARCH errors.

We now have expressions for the variance of the l-steps-ahead forecast error for the previously discussed RCA(1)-GARCH(p,q)x$(P,Q)_s$ models:

RCA(1)-GARCH$(0,1)$x$(0,1)_s$ $\quad \text{Var}[e_n^{(Y)}(l)] = \dfrac{(K^{(\epsilon)}-1)\mu^2}{(1+\theta^2)(1+\Theta^2)} \sum_{j=0}^{l-1} \Psi_j^2$

RCA(1)-GARCH$(0,1)$x$(1,0)_s$ $\quad \text{Var}[e_n^{(Y)}(l)] = \dfrac{(K^{(\epsilon)}-1)\mu^2(1-\Phi^2)}{1+\theta^2} \sum_{j=0}^{l-1} \Psi_j^2$

RCA(1)-GARCH$(1,0)$x$(1,0)_s$ $\quad \text{Var}[e_n^{(Y)}(l)] = \dfrac{(K^{(\epsilon)}-1)\mu^2(1-\phi^2)}{1+2\phi^s\Phi+\Phi^2} \sum_{j=0}^{l-1} \Psi_j^2$

which are similar to the expressions given in Doshi et al. (2011). Here, $K^{(\epsilon)}$ is given in Theorem 4.2. and expressions for $K^{(y)}$ for a conditionally normally distributed ϵ_t are given in Examples 4.1, 4.2, and 4.3.

5. RCA models with seasonal SV errors

We start with Taylor's (2005) stochastic volatility (SV) model and propose its seasonal form,

$$y_t = (\beta + b_t)y_{t-1} + \epsilon_t \tag{24}$$

$$\epsilon_t = Z_t e^{\frac{1}{2}h_t} \qquad Z_t \sim N(0,1) \tag{25}$$

$$\phi(B)\Phi(L)h_t = \omega + v_t \qquad v_t \sim N(0, \sigma_v^2) \tag{26}$$

where ϵ_t and h_t are innovations of the observed time series y_t and the unobserved stochastic volatility, respectively. Also, $\phi(B) = 1 - \sum_{i=1}^{q} \phi_i B^i$, $\Phi(L) = 1 - \sum_{i=1}^{Q} \Phi_i L^i$, and $L = B^s$, where s is the seasonal period. We assume that all the zeros of the polynomial $\phi(B)\Phi(L)$ lie outside the unit circle; thus, h_t as given in (26) is stationary. The moving average representation is $h_t = \omega + \sum_{j=0}^{\infty} \Psi_j v_{t-j}$ where $\{\Psi_j\}$ is a sequence of constants and $\sum_{j=0}^{\infty} \Psi_j^2 < \infty$. The Ψ_j's are obtained from $\phi(B)\Phi(L)\Psi(B) = 1$ where $\Psi(B) = 1 + \sum_{j=1}^{\infty} \Psi_j B^j$.

RCA models with SV innovations have been studied in Paseka et al. (2010). Here we consider the seasonal version of the SV process and we study the moment properties of RCA models with seasonal SV innovations.

Theorem 5.1. Suppose y_t is an RCA model with seasonal SV innovations as in (24)– (26). Then, we have the following relationship:

(i) $E(y_t^2) = \dfrac{E(\epsilon_t^2)}{1 - (\beta^2 + \sigma_b^2)}$,

(ii) $E(y_t^4) = \dfrac{6(\sigma_b^2 + \beta^2)[E(\epsilon_t^2)]^2 + [1 - (\beta^2 + \sigma_b^2)]E(\epsilon_t^4)}{1 - (3\sigma_b^4 + \beta^4 + 6\beta^2\sigma_b^2)[1 - (\beta^2 + \sigma_b^2)]}$,

(iii) $K^{(y)} = \dfrac{6(\sigma_b^2 + \beta^2)[1 - (\beta^2 + \sigma_b^2)]}{1 - (3\sigma_b^4 + \beta^4 + 6\beta^2\sigma_b^2)} + \dfrac{[1 - (\beta^2 + \sigma_b^2)]^2}{1 - (3\sigma_b^4 + \beta^4 + 6\beta^2\sigma_b^2)} K^{(\epsilon)}$,

(iv) $K^{(\epsilon)} = 3e^{\sigma_v^2 \sum_{j=0}^{\infty} \Psi_j^2}$

where $E(\epsilon_t^2) = \exp\left\{\mu_{h_t} + \frac{1}{2}\sigma_{h_t}^2\right\}$, $E(\epsilon_t^4) = 3\exp\left\{2\mu_{h_t} + 2\sigma_{h_t}^2\right\}$, the mean of the h_t process is $\mu_{h_t} = \dfrac{\omega}{(1 - \sum_{i=1}^{q} \phi_i)(1 - \sum_{i=1}^{Q} \Phi_i)}$ and the variance of h_t is $\sigma_{h_t}^2 = \sigma_v^2 \sum_{j=0}^{\infty} \Psi_j^2$.

Proof. Parts (i) to (iii) are similar to Paseka et al. (2010) for an RCA-non seasonal SV process. Part (iv) follows from the above expressions for $E(\epsilon_t^2)$ and $E(\epsilon_t^4)$ as follows:

$$K^{(\epsilon)} = \frac{E(\epsilon_t^4)}{[E(\epsilon_t^2)]^2} = \frac{3e^{2\mu_{h_t} + 2\sigma_{h_t}^2}}{(e^{\mu_{h_t} + 1/2\sigma_{h_t}^2})2} = 3e^{\sigma_{h_t}^2} = 3e^{\sigma_v^2 \sum_{j=0}^{\infty} \Psi_j^2}.$$

Next, we illustrate applications of Theorem 5.1 with three examples.

Example 5.1. RCA with autoregressive [AR(1)] SV process

$$y_t = (\beta + b_t)y_{t-1} + \epsilon_t$$

$$\epsilon_t = Z_t e^{\frac{1}{2}h_t}$$

$$(1 - \phi B)h_t = \omega + v_t$$

The Ψ-weights are $\Psi_j = \phi^j, j \geq 1$. Therefore, $\sum_{j=0}^{\infty} \Psi_j^2 = 1 + \phi^2 + \phi^4 + \ldots = \frac{1}{1-\phi^2}$. Then, the kurtosis of y_t is:

$$K^{(y)} = \frac{6(\sigma_b^2+\beta^2)[1-(\beta^2+\sigma_b^2)]}{1-(3\sigma_b^4+\beta^4+6\beta^2\sigma_b^2)} + 3\frac{[1-(\beta^2+\sigma_b^2)]^2}{1-(3\sigma_b^4+\beta^4+6\beta^2\sigma_b^2)}\exp\left\{\frac{\sigma_v^2}{1-\phi^2}\right\}.$$

Example 5.2. RCA with pure seasonal autoregressive [AR$(1)_s$] SV process

$$\begin{aligned} y_t &= (\beta + b_t)y_{t-1} + \epsilon_t \\ \epsilon_t &= Z_t e^{\frac{1}{2}h_t} \\ (1-\Phi B^s)h_t &= \omega + v_t \end{aligned}$$

The Ψ-weights are $\Psi_j = \Phi^j, j \geq 1$. Therefore, $\sum_{j=0}^{\infty} \Psi_j^2 = 1 + \Phi^2 + \Phi^4 + \ldots = \frac{1}{1-\Phi^2}$. Then, the kurtosis of y_t is:

$$K^{(y)} = \frac{6(\sigma_b^2+\beta^2)[1-(\beta^2+\sigma_b^2)]}{1-(3\sigma_b^4+\beta^4+6\beta^2\sigma_b^2)} + 3\frac{[1-(\beta^2+\sigma_b^2)]^2}{1-(3\sigma_b^4+\beta^4+6\beta^2\sigma_b^2)}\exp\left\{\frac{\sigma_v^2}{1-\Phi^2}\right\}.$$

Example 5.3. RCA with multiplicative seasonal autoregressive [AR(1)x$(1)_s$] SV process

$$\begin{aligned} y_t &= (\beta + b_t)y_{t-1} + \epsilon_t \\ \epsilon_t &= Z_t e^{\frac{1}{2}h_t} \\ (1-\phi B)(1-\Phi B^s)h_t &= \omega + v_t \end{aligned}$$

The Ψ-weights are $\Psi_1 = \phi + \Phi$, and $\Psi_j = (\phi + \Phi)\Psi_{j-1} + \phi\Phi\Psi_{j-2}, j \geq 2$. Then, the kurtosis of y_t is:

$$K^{(y)} = \frac{6(\sigma_b^2+\beta^2)[1-(\beta^2+\sigma_b^2)]}{1-(3\sigma_b^4+\beta^4+6\beta^2\sigma_b^2)} + 3\frac{[1-(\beta^2+\sigma_b^2)]^2}{1-(3\sigma_b^4+\beta^4+6\beta^2\sigma_b^2)}e^{\sigma_{h_t}^2}$$

where $\sigma_{h_t}^2 = \frac{(1+\phi^s)\sigma_v^2}{(1-\phi^2)(1-\Phi^2)(1-\Phi\phi^s)}$.

Recently, Gong & Thavaneswaran (2009) discussed the filtering of SV models. The prediction of discrete SV models can be obtained by using the recursive method proposed in Gong & Thavaneswaran (2009).

6. Option pricing with seasonal volatility

Option pricing based on the Black-Scholes model is widely used in the financial community. The Black-Scholes formula is used for the pricing of European-style options. The model has traditionally assumed that the volatility of returns is constant. However, several studies have shown that asset returns exhibit variances that change over time. Duan (1995) proposes an option pricing model for an asset with returns following a GARCH process. Badescu & Kulpeger (2008); Elliot et al. (2006); Heston & Nandi (2000) and others derived closed form option pricing formulas for different models which are assumed to follow a GARCH volatility process. Most recently, Gong et al. (2010) derive an expression for the call price as an expectation with respect to random GARCH volatility. The model is then evaluated in terms of the moments of the volatility process. Their results indicate that the suggested model outperforms the classic Black-Scholes formula. Here we extend Gong et al. (2010) and propose an option pricing model with seasonal GARCH volatility as follows:

$$dS_t = rS_t dt + \sigma_t S_t dW_t \tag{27}$$

$$y_t = \log\left(\frac{S_t}{S_{t-1}}\right) - E\left[\log\left(\frac{S_t}{S_{t-1}}\right)\right] = \sigma_t Z_t \tag{28}$$

$$\theta(B)\Theta(L)\sigma_t^2 = \omega + \alpha(B)y_t^2 \tag{29}$$

where S_t is the price of the stock, r is the risk-free interest rate, $\{W_t\}$ is a standard Brownian motion, σ_t is the time-varying seasonal volatility process, $\{Z_t\}$ is a sequence of i.i.d. random variables with zero mean and unit variance and $\alpha(B)$, $\theta(B)$ and $\Theta(L)$ have been defined in (4).

The price of a call option can be calculated using the option pricing formula given in Gong et al. (2010). The call price is derived as a first conditional moment of a truncated lognormal distribution under the martingale measure, and it is based on estimates of the moments of the GARCH process. The call price based on the Black-Scholes model with seasonal GARCH volatility is given by:

$$\begin{aligned} C(S,T) &= S\left(f[E(\sigma_t^2)] + \frac{1}{2}f''[E(\sigma_t^2)]\left(\frac{1}{3}\kappa^{(y)} - 1\right)E^2(\sigma_t^2)\right) \\ &\quad - Ke^{-rT}\left(g[E(\sigma_t^2)] + \frac{1}{2}g''[E(\sigma_t^2)]\left(\frac{1}{3}\kappa^{(y)} - 1\right)E^2(\sigma_t^2)\right), \end{aligned} \tag{30}$$

where f and g are twice differentiable functions, S is the initial value of S_t, K is the strike price, T is the expiry date, σ_t is a stationary process with finite fourth moment, and $\kappa^{(y)} = \frac{E(y_t^4)}{[E(y_t^2)]^2}$. Also, $f[E(\sigma_t^2)]$, $g[E(\sigma_t^2)]$, $f''[E(\sigma_t^2)]$, and $g''[E(\sigma_t^2)]$ are given by:

$$f[E(\sigma_t^2)] = \mathrm{N}(d) = \mathrm{N}\left(\frac{\log(S/K) + rT + \frac{1}{2}E(\sigma_t^2)}{\sqrt{E(\sigma_t^2)}}\right),$$

$$g[E(\sigma_t^2)] = \mathrm{N}\left(d - \sqrt{E(\sigma_t^2)}\right) = \mathrm{N}\left(\frac{\log(S/K) + rT - \frac{1}{2}E(\sigma_t^2)}{\sqrt{E(\sigma_t^2)}}\right),$$

$$\begin{aligned} f''[E(\sigma_t^2)] = \frac{1}{\sqrt{2\pi}}\Bigg[&- \left(\frac{E(\sigma_t^2) - 2(\log(S/K) + rT)}{4E(\sigma_t^2)\sqrt{E(\sigma_t^2)}}\right)\left(\frac{[E(\sigma_t^2)]^2 - 4(\log(S/K) + rT)^2}{8[E(\sigma_t^2)]^2}\right) \\ &+ \left(\frac{6(\log(S/K) + rT) - E(\sigma_t^2)}{8[E(\sigma_t^2)]^2\sqrt{E(\sigma_t^2)}}\right)\Bigg] \times \exp\left\{-\frac{(2(\log(S/K) + rT) + E(\sigma_t^2))^2}{8E(\sigma_t^2)}\right\}, \end{aligned}$$

$$g''[E(\sigma_t^2)] = \frac{1}{\sqrt{2\pi}}\left[\left(\frac{E(\sigma_t^2)+2(\log(S/K)+rT)}{4E(\sigma_t^2)\sqrt{E(\sigma_t^2)}}\right)\left(\frac{[E(\sigma_t^2)]^2-4(\log(S/K)+rT)^2}{[E(\sigma_t^2)]^2}\right)\right.$$
$$\left.+\left(\frac{6(\log(S/K)+rT)+E(\sigma_t^2)}{8[E(\sigma_t^2)]^2\sqrt{E(\sigma_t^2)}}\right)\right]\exp\left\{-\frac{(2(\log(S/K)+rT)-E(\sigma_t^2))^2}{8E(\sigma_t^2)}\right\},$$

where N denotes the standard normal CDF, and under the option pricing model with seasonal GARCH volatility,

$$E(\sigma_t^2) = \frac{\omega}{\left(1-\sum_{i=1}^{p}\phi_i\right)\left(1-\sum_{i=1}^{P}\Phi_i\right)},$$
$$\kappa^{(y)} = \frac{3}{3-2\sum_{j=1}^{\infty}\Psi_j^2}.$$

7. Concluding remarks

In this chapter we propose various classes of seasonal volatility models. We consider time series processes such as AR and RCA with multiplicative seasonal GARCH errors and SV errors. The multiplicative seasonal volatility models are suitable for time series where autocorrelation exists at seasonal and at adjacent non-seasonal lags. The models introduced here extend and complement the existing volatility models in the literature to seasonal volatility models by introducing more general structures.

It is well-known that financial time series exhibit excess kurtosis. In this chapter we derive the kurtosis for different seasonal volatility models in terms of model parameters. We also derive the closed-from expression for the variance of the l-steps ahead forecast error of i) y_{n+l} in terms of ψ-weights and model parameters, and of ii) squared series Y_{n+l} in terms of Ψ-weights, model parameters and the kurtosis of ϵ_t. The results are a generalization of existing results for non-seasonal volatility processes. We provide examples for all the different classes of models considered and discussed them in some detail (i.e. AR(1)-GARCH$(p,q) \times (P,Q)_s$, RCA(1)-GARCH$(p,q) \times (P,Q)_s$ and RCA(1)-seasonal SV).

The results are primarily oriented to financial time series applications. Financial time series often meet the large dataset demands of the volatility models studied here. Also, financial data dynamics in higher order moments are of interest to many market participants. Specifically, we consider the Black-Scholes model with seasonal GARCH volatility and show that the moments of the seasonal volatility process can be used to evaluate the call price for European options.

8. References

Badescu, A. & Kulperger, R. (2008). GARCH option pricing: A semiparametric approach. *Insurance, Mathematics & Economics*, Vol. 43, No. 1, 69 – 84, ISSN 0167-6687

Baillie, R. & Bollerslev, T. (1990). Intra-day and inter-market volatility in foreign exchange rates. *Review of Economic Studies*, Vol. 58, No. 3, 565 – 585, ISSN 0034-6527

Bollerslev, T. (1986). Generalized autoregressive conditional heteroscedasticity. *Journal of Econometrics*, Vol. 31, 307 – 327, ISSN 0304-4076

Bollerslev, T. & Ghysels, E. (1996). Periodic autoregressive conditional heteroscedasticity. *Journal of Business and Economic Statistics*, Vol. 14, No. 2, 139 – 151, ISSN: 0735-0015

Doshi, A.; Frank, J.; Thavaneswaran, A. (2011). Seasonal volatility models. *Journal of Statistical Theory and Applications*, Vol. 10, No. 1, 1–10, ISSN 1538-7887

Duan, J. (1995). The GARCH option ricing model. *Mathematical Finance*, Vol. 5, 13–32, ISSN 0960-1627

Elliot, R.; Siu, T.; Chan, L. (2006). Option pricing for GARCH models with Markov switching. *International Journal of Theoretical and Applied Finance*, Vol. 9, No. 6, 825–841, ISSN 0219-0249

Engle, R. (1982). Autoregressive conditional heteroskedasticity with estimates of the variance of U.K. inflation. *Econometrica*, Vol. 50, 987–1008, ISSN 0012-9682

Frank, J. & Garcia, P. (2009). Time-varying risk premium: further evidence in agricultural futures markets. *Applied Economics*, Vol. 41, No. 6, 715 – 725, ISSN 0003-6846

Franses, P. & Paap, R. (2000). Modelling day-of-the-week seasonality in the S&P 500 index. *Applied Financial Economics*, Vol. 10, No. 5, 483 – 488, ISSN 0960-3107

Ghahramani, M. & Thavaneswaran, A. (2007). Identification of ARMA models with GARCH errors. *The Mathematical Scientist*, Vol. 32, No. 1, 60 – 69, ISSN 0312-3685

Ghysels, E. & Osborn, D. (2001). *The econometric analysis of seasonal time series*, Cambridge University Press, ISBN 0-521-56588-X, United Kingdom.

Gong, H. & Thavaneswaran, A. (2009). Recursive estimation for continuous time stochastic volatility models. *Applied Mathematics Letters*, Vol. 22, No. 11, 1770 – 1774, ISSN 0893-9659

Gong, H.; Thavaneswaran, A.; Singh, J. (2010). A Black-Scholes model with GARCH volatility. *The Mathematical Scientist*, Vol. 35, No. 1, 37–42, ISSN 0312-3685

Heston, S. & Nandi, S. (2000). A closed-form GARCH option valuation model. *The Review of Financial Studies*, Vol. 13, No. 3, 585 – 625, ISSN 0893-9454

Nicholls, D. & Quinn, B. (1982). Random coefficient autoregressive models: An introduction. *Lecture Notes in Statistics*, Vol. 11, Springer, ISSN 0930-0325, New York.

Paseka, A.; Appadoo, S.; Thavaneswaran, A. (2010). Random coefficient autoregressive (RCA) models with nonlinear stochastic volatility innovations. *Journal of Applied Statistical Science*, Vol. 17, No. 3, 331–349, ISSN 1067-5817

Taylor, S. (2005). *Asset price dynamics, volatility, and prediction*, Princeton University Press, ISBN 0-691-11537-0, New Jersey.

Thavaneswaran, A. & Ghahramani, M. (2008). Volatility forecasts with GARCH errors and applications. *Journal of Statistical Theory and Applications*, Vol. 1, No. 1, 69 – 80, ISSN 1538-7887

Thavaneswaran, A.; Appadoo, S.; Ghahramani, M. (2009). RCA models with GARCH innovations. *Applied Mathematics Letters*, Vol. 22, 110–114, ISSN 0893-9659

Thavaneswaran, A.; Appadoo, S.; Peiris, S. (2005a). Forecasting volatility. *Statistics and Probability Letters*, Vol. 75, No. 1, 1–10, ISSN: 0167-7152

Thavaneswaran, A.; Appadoo, S.; Samanta, M. (2005b). Random coefficient GARCH Models. *Mathematical and Computer Modelling*, Vol. 41, No. 1–7, 723–733, ISSN 0895-7177

Part 2

Recent Econometric Applications

4

The Impact of Government-Sponsored Training Programs on the Labor Market Transitions of Disadvantaged Men

Lucie Gilbert[1], Thierry Kamionka[2] and Guy Lacroix[3]
[1]*Human Resources Development Canada*
[2]*CREST, CNRS*
[3]*CIRPÉE, CIRANO, IZA, Laval University*
[1,3]*Canada*
[2]*France*

1. Introduction

The impact of government-sponsored training programs has been extensively studied in the past couple of decades.[1] In many countries, such programs have become an integral part of public policies aiming at enhancing self-sufficiency among vulnerable groups. In most cases program costs have escalated as they have become more comprehensive and more systematically used. Not surprisingly, policy makers have shown renewed interest in obtaining accurate and reliable estimates of their efficacy.

The discussions surrounding the efficacy or desirability of training programs rest on complex methodological issues. The main concern lies with proper treatment of an individual's decision to participate in such programs. Severe biases may arise if unobserved individual characteristics that affect the decision to participate are somehow related to the unobservables that affect outcomes on the labour market. Two approaches have been proposed in the evaluation literature to address the so-called "self-selection" issue. The first is the "experimental approach", based on random assignment of applicants into treatment or control groups. The second is the "non experimental", or "econometric approach", and relies on non-random samples of participants and non-participants. Each approach tackles the self-selection issue from a different angle, but the relative merit of each is still the subject of debate [see Heckman & Smith (1995), Burtless (1995), Ham & LaLonde (1996), Keane (2010), Leamer (2010)].

Most would argue that the "experimental" approach is best suited to eliminate self-selection biases and provide adequate mean program impacts, however measured. Yet, recently this view has been challenged by Ham & LaLonde (1996) in their important paper.[2] In essence they argue that random assignment between control and experimental groups provides an

[1] See Heckman et al. (1999) for a detailed survey.

[2] A number of papers have found evidence of biases in randomized field experiments. See Card & Hyslop (2005), Card & Hyslop (2009), Brouillette & Lacroix (2010), Kamionka & Lacroix (2008), Crépon et al. (2011).

adequate *short-term* mean program impact. On the other hand, the treatment and controls experiencing subsequent spells of employment and unemployment are most likely not random subsets of the initial groups because the sorting process is very different for the two. In other words, random assignment does not guarantee that long-term mean program impacts are void of any systematic biases.

In most countries, experimental evaluation of training programs is impracticable due to a lack of appropriate data. Analysts must rely on multi-state transition models. An additional difficulty in using these data is that program participation must be modeled explicitly. Many recent papers have nevertheless managed to successfully model complex transition patterns using such data (Gritz (1993), Bonnal et al. (1997), Mealli et al. (1996), Brouillette & Lacroix (2011), Fougère et al. (2010), Blasco, Crépon & Kamionka (2009)). Most papers are limited to three separate states of the labour market: employment, unemployment (non-employment) and training.[3] In many cases data limitations do not allow identification of any more states. In other cases, analysts purposely focus on few states to keep the statistical model tractable. Indeed, when the data is drawn from stock samples, as is often the case when using administrative data, the statistical model must account for so-called "initial conditions" problems. This usually adds considerable complexity to an already involved statistical model.[4] On the other hand, many have questioned the appropriateness of focusing on few labour market states (Heckman & Flinn (1983), Jones & Riddell (1999)).

This chapter investigates the impact of government training programs aimed at poorly educated Canadian male welfare recipients. It should be stressed at the outset that in Canada, as in many European countries, the welfare system aims at supporting individuals without income and who are not entitled to any other social security benefits, irrespective of age.[5] As such, it acts as a safety net for unemployed workers who do not qualify for benefits, or who have exhausted their unemployment benefits. Many programs are available to assist these long term unemployed and those with few skills increase their employability. Understandably, a considerable proportion of program resources has been targeted towards the youths in the past decade. Yet, many have questioned the ability of traditional programs to address the problem [OECD, 1998]. The aim of this chapter is precisely to investigate the impact of these programs in enhancing the self-sufficiency of young males welfare claimants, a particular disadvantaged group (see Beaudry & Green (2000)).

The empirical strategy is similar to that used by Gritz (1993), Bonnal et al. (1997) and Brouillette & Lacroix (2011) in that we explicitly account for selectivity into the training programs. It relies on a rich dataset that tracks the transitions of a large number of individuals on a weekly basis across seven different states of the labour market. These states include employment, unemployment, welfare, out of the labour force (OLF), two separate welfare training programs, and unemployment training programs. In all, as many as 24 different transitions are allowed in the model. The sample is drawn from the population of welfare

[3] One notable exception is Bonnal et al. (1997) who consider as many as 6 different different states: permanent employment, temporary employment, public policy employment (training), unemployment, out-of-labour-force (non-employment), and an absorbing state (attrition).

[4] Two biases are likely to result from stock samples: (1) length-bias; (2) inflow-rate bias. The former may arise because lengthy spells are more likely to be ongoing at the time the sample is chosen. The latter is related to the fact that the probability of being sampled is related to the probability of starting a fresh spell at time the sample is chosen. See Gouriéroux & Monfort (1992) and Van den Berg et al. (1994) for a detailed analysis.

[5] Individuals must be aged over 18 to qualify for benefits, although single parents less than 18 still qualify.

recipients that experienced a spell at any time between 1987 and 1993 in the province of Québec, Canada. To be included in the sample, individuals had to be aged 18 or 19 at any time during that period and to have less than a high-school degree. Sample stratification is used to avoid over-parameterization of the statistical model that would result if too many exogenous variables had to be controlled for.

By merging various administrative data files we can recreate complete individuals' histories on the labour market back to age 16, the legal school-leaving age in Canada. Consequently, each individual in our sample is necessarily observed in the OLF state at the beginning of his history. This sampling scheme thus removes the necessity to control for stock sample biases and has the additional benefit of providing rich transition patterns over a relatively long sample frame.

The econometric model is built on continuous labour market transitions processes and allows entry rates into each state to depend on observed and unobserved heterogeneity components. Heterogeneity terms can be destination-specific, origin-specific or both. In all cases, correlation across heterogeneity terms is allowed. We further investigate the sensitivity of the parameter estimates to various distributions of the heterogeneity components. When parametric distribution functions are used, the model is estimated by Simulated Maximum Likelihood (SML).

The remainder of the chapter is organized as follows. Section 2 provides a detailed description of the data. Section 3 discusses the econometric model and the various statistical assumption regarding the distributions of the heterogeneity terms. Section 4 reports our empirical findings. Section 5 concludes the chapter.

2. Data description

The basic data used for this study are drawn from the caseload records of Québec's Ministère de la Solidarité sociale. The files contain information on all individuals who have received welfare benefits at some time between January 1987 and December 1993. In particular, the start dates and end dates of each welfare and welfare training spells are recorded in the files. The welfare program contains special provisions for those who are indisposed for work due to mental or physical impediments. These individuals are not included in the sample. Thus the final sample comprises only individuals who have no handicap or only a minor, intermediate, or temporary physical handicap. Furthermore, they are fit to work.

The welfare administrative files contain no information on employment or unemployment spells. Our sample was thus linked to the Status Vector files (SV) and the Record of Employment (ROE) files, both under the aegis of Human Resources Development Canada. These files contain very detailed weekly information on insured unemployment spells and employment spells, respectively. The start dates and end dates of each spell are recorded in these files. Similar information is available with respect to training spells administered under the Unemployment Insurance (UI) program. Merging all three administrative files allows us to define seven different states on the labour market. Aside from the welfare, unemployment and employment states, we can identify two separate welfare training states and one unemployment training state.[6]

The focus of this chapter is on poorly educated young men. Thus to be included in the sample, an individual had to be either 18 or 19 years of age at any time between 1987 and 1993 and have completed less than 11 years of schooling over the sample period. A high-school degree in Québec usually entails at least 12 years of schooling. In principle, then, none of the individuals in our sample has earned a high-school diploma. With these selection criteria the final sample contains 3068 individuals.

The upper panel of Table 1 provides summary statistics for individuals who have not participated in a training program. The lower panel presents similar statistics for program participants. In the latter case, the mean durations in either employment, unemployment or welfare are calculated both before and after training. An examination of the table reveals that the two groups are very similar in terms of their observable characteristics; They both have the same average age and nearly identical schooling levels. Yet, there are significant differences in their respective labour market experiences. For instance, non-trainees have longer spells in each of the three states reported in the table. On the whole, the proportion of time non-trainees spend employed is slightly larger than that of trainees prior to training. On the other hand, once they have had training, the proportion of time trainees spend employed becomes larger than that of non-trainees. This increase stems from the fact that the average employment duration decreases proportionately less that the average duration of welfare and unemployment spells. Taken at face value, this would suggest training programs benefit somewhat to welfare recipients.

Recall that only individuals who experienced a welfare spell between 1987 and 1993 and who were aged 18 or 19 during that period are included in the sample. Those who are 18 or 19 years of age in January 1987 may have already been on the labour market for 2–3 years at most. In order to recreate their complete labour market histories as of the age of 16, it is necessary in some cases to go back as early as January 1984.[7] The start date and end date of each spell is used to create individual histories on the labour market. Overlaps between states are frequent and are not necessarily the result of coding errors. It may well be, for example, that a welfare spell and a work spell overlap. Program designs do not forbid this. In principle, such overlaps could be redefined as a separate state. Given the number of possible states, it is simply not

[6] The welfare files contain information dating back to 1979 and ending in December 1993. The SV files contains information beginning in January 1987 and ending in December 1996. Finally, The ROE files contain information ranging from January 1975 to December 1996. The analysis focuses on the 1987–1993 period due to data limitations.

[7] Data concerning unemployment spells are available only as of January 1987. Consequently, a small proportion of unemployment spells occurring prior to 1987 may be wrongly coded as out of the labour force (OLF). Two factors lead us to believe that the proportion of such spells is likely insignificant. First, the large majority of individuals who were 18 or 19 years of age in the years 1990 and beyond where in the OLF, the employment or the welfare states between 16 and 19. Second, of those individuals, the majority who had an employment spell would not have qualified for UI benefits given the eligibility rules that prevailed between 1984 and 1987.

A similar problem arises with respect to employment spells. Indeed, spells that were ongoing in December 1993 will not show up in the ROE files until they are terminated. To avoid misclassifying these spells as OLF, the ROE files are searched as late as December 1996. Given the average length of employment spells reported in Table 1, it is very unlikely that many employment spells that were ongoing in December 1993 will still be ongoing as late as December 1996, and thus wrongly classified as OLF.

	Mean	Std. dev.	Mean	Std. dev.
Individual without training				
Age when entering the sample	19.92	1.84		
Education	9.84	1.03		
Duration of employment episodes (weeks)†	26.15	30.47		
Duration of welfare episodes (weeks)†	35.63	34.43		
Duration of unemployment episodes (weeks)†	39.90	11.99		
Duration of OLF episodes (weeks)†	42.99	50.95		
Proportion of time employed (weeks)‡	0.18			
Number of observations	1165			
Individual with training				
Age when entering the sample	19.77	(1.95)		
Education	9.72	(1.03)		
	Before training		*After training*	
Duration of employment episodes (weeks)†	24.26	37.13	17.44	18.25
Duration of welfare episodes (weeks)†	54.90	54.86	35.14	51.09
Duration of unemployment episodes (weeks)†	41.25	14.41	35.73	16.83
Duration of OLF episodes (weeks)†	30.78	38.86	18.66	21.16
Proportion of time employed (weeks)‡	0.17		0.16	
Number of observations	1903			

Table 1. Sample Characteristics

† *Calculated from non censored episodes.*

‡ *Calculated from mean duration in employment, unemployment, welfare and OLF.*

reasonable to allow these overlaps in the analysis. It was decided that, as a rule, starting dates would have precedence over ongoing spells. Thus an ongoing spell with known end date is truncated whenever a new state starts prior to the end date.[8]

The 3 068 individuals in our sample experienced as many as 31 422 spells over the sample period. Table 2 presents all the transitions that occurred at any given point in the sample period. The table identifies seven separate states on the labour market. Welfare Training includes various job search assistance programs as well as skill enhancing programs aimed at welfare recipients. The Job-Reentry Program (JRP) is an on-the-job training program also aimed at welfare recipients. Under this program, participants do not receive benefits but a (subsidized) salary from a regular employer.[9] JRP is treated separately because contrary to other programs most participants qualify for unemployment benefits upon completion. UI is a state in which individuals receive unemployment benefits. Individuals that do not work and that do not qualify for benefits are treated as out of the labour force (OLF) for the purpose of this study. It must thus be kept in mind that UI is not necessarily akin to unemployment in the usual sense. UI Training comprises a series of training programs aimed at UI claimants. The OLF state is the complement of all other states. It includes full-time students, non-entitled unemployed individuals and individuals that are truly out of the labour force.

Table 2 reveals interesting dynamics on the labour market. For instance, the majority of welfare spells end either in employment, in welfare training or OLF. Likewise, welfare training spells end either in welfare, in employment or in OLF. Interestingly, most JRP participants enter regular employment upon completion of their program. Very few enter UI even though

[8] Preliminary analysis was also conducted giving the end date precedence over the start date of a new spell. The resulting transitions matrices and average durations are very robust to this strategy.

[9] Non-profit organizations have to pay a symbolic 1$ per working day. The participants receive regular benefits.

Destination / *Origin*	Welfare	Welfare Training	JRP	U.I.	U.I. Training	Employment	OLF
Welfare	0	1809	140	88	0	1851	1134
Welfare Training	432	0	67	6	0	438	306
JRP	21	4	0	7	0	192	29
U.I.	374	38	2	292	111	1380	1404
U.I. Training	2	1	0	114	0	16	2
Employment	1002	229	35	2918	41	2004	4662
OLF	2614	235	9	523	2	3815	0

Table 2. Frequency of Transitions Between States

most qualify for benefits. Other transitions are as expected, except perhaps for UI training. Indeed, the majority of participants return to UI upon completion of their program and very few find regular employment. A number of cells contain few or no observations. The empty cells are consistent with program or policy parameters that prevent a number of transitions to occur or are a consequence of our definitions of the various states.[10] Only transitions comprising more than 75 observations will be considered in the econometric model. This leaves a total of 24 transitions to be modeled explicitly.

The transitions on the labour market have three essential dimensions: the state of origin, the state of destination and the duration in any a given state. Table 2 provides useful information on the first two dimensions. One way to represent all three dimensions simultaneously is to look at the distribution of the sample across all seven states on a weekly basis. This distribution synthesizes both the transitions across states and the mean duration in each.

Figure 1 plots the proportion of individuals in each of the seven states on a weekly basis. The top portion of the figure traces out the proportion of individuals in non-training states (welfare, unemployment, employment, OLF), and the bottom portion traces out the proportions in training states (UI training, welfare training and JRP). There are two distinct features that arise in January 1987 in the top portion of the figure. First, the proportion of individuals in OLF is relatively high. This partly reflects a cohort effect. In January 1987, our sample comprises only individuals that are 18 or 19 years of age. Not surprisingly, a large proportion of them are either still in school or have not yet entered the labour market. As we move rightward along the time axis, these individuals become older and new 18-19 year old entrants join the sample. By the time we reach December 1993, the oldest individuals are between 25–26 years of age. It does not necessarily follow that the sample's average age increases systematically along the time axis. Proportionately more individuals have entered the sample in the recession years 1989–1992 than previously. Second, the proportion of unemployed individuals is zero. As mentioned earlier, the information on unemployment spells is only available as of January 1987. Consequently, only new spells are identifiable in the data. Spells that were ongoing in January 1987 are classified as OLF in the figure.

The bottom portion of the figure also indicates that the proportion of individuals in JRP is zero up until approximately January-February 1990. This program was implemented in August

[10] For example, the welfare files provide information on a monthly basis. Any interruption lasting between 1-3 weeks will not be recorded in the data. The record will show an uninterrupted sequence of monthly benefits receipt. Thus Welfare-Welfare transitions are not identifiable in the data. On the other hand, UI spells are recorded on a weekly basis. Unemployed workers that work a number of weeks or hours while claiming benefits may qualify for additional benefits once they exhaust their original entitlement. The SV files will indicate a new UI spell starting the week following exhaustion. Thus UI-UI transitions are identifiable in the data.

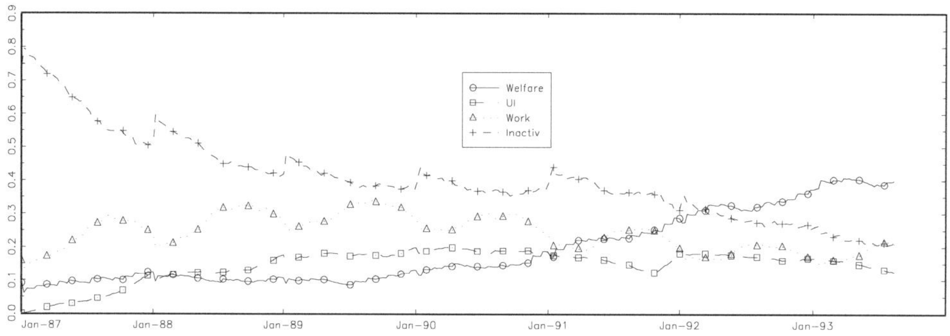

Fig. 1. Distribution Across States

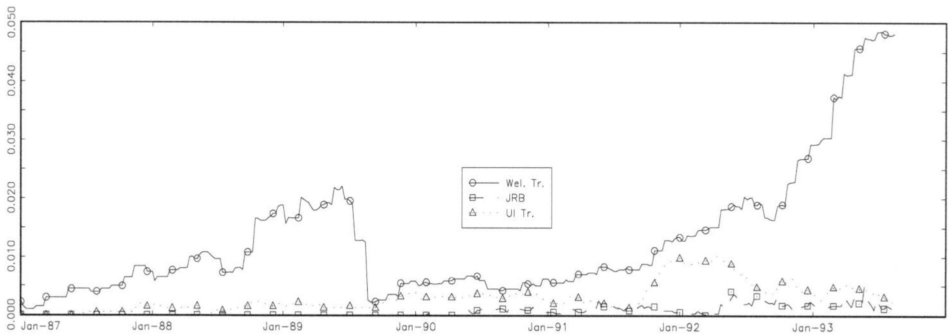

Fig. 2. Distribution Across Training Programs

1989 and had too few participants in the beginning months to show up in the figure. Similarly, participation in UI training programs is essentially zero up until February-March 1987. UI training usually occurs after a number of weeks has been spent unemployed. Not surprisingly, then, a certain laps of time is needed before the proportion of UI trainees is large enough to show up in the figure. Training spells that were ongoing in January 1987 are also classified as OLF.

A close look at Figure 1 reveals interesting patterns. First, the proportion of welfare participants remains relatively constant between 1987 and 1989. The economic downturn of 1989 results in an steady increase in the proportion of welfare claimants until the end of 1993. In fact, the proportion increased from 17.9% in January 1988 to 42.3% in December 1993. Such an increase results from both a more important inflow into welfare and longer spell duration [see Duclos et al. (1999) for details].

The proportion of employed individuals follows a very distinct seasonal pattern with peaks occurring around June-July and troughs around January of each year. Despite these seasonal fluctuations, the proportion of employed individuals increased from 31.2% in January 1988 to 33.5% in January 1990, and then gradually declined to 18.6% in January 1993. The proportion of unemployed individuals is highly negatively correlated with the proportion of employed individuals. The seasonal fluctuations almost perfectly mirror those of employment. Finally, the proportion of individuals in the OLF state also depicts strong seasonal patterns. In January of each year, the proportion of those in OLF increases by about 5 percentage points. It is likely that many seasonal workers lose their job at the beginning of each year and do not qualify for unemployment benefits.

The bottom portion of the figure shows that the proportion of individuals engaged in government-sponsored training programs fluctuates considerably over time. A number of new welfare training programs have been implemented in 1989. Most of these programs aim at enhancing job search skills and usually last a few weeks. The large increase in the proportion of welfare trainees coincide with the implementation of these programs. A dramatic fall occurs towards the end of 1989 presumably linked to budgetary constraints associated with the economic downturn of 1990. The proportion of participants steadily increases thereafter and reaches its peak at the end of 1993. The proportion of UI trainees is relatively constant throughout the whole period, with the exception of 1992. Both the UI training programs and JRP have relatively few participants at any point in time.

The proportions of participants in the combined programs hardly reach beyond 5% over the sample period. The fact that few individuals are engaged in formal training at any point in time is no indication that training programs are inefficient or unattractive. Access to programs is often limited because of insufficient resources. This lack of resources raises a fundamental question: who gets selected into training? To the econometrician, participation in a training program is the result of two separate unidentifiable processes. First, the participant has undertaken the necessary steps to take part in the program. Second, the program manager has deemed the participant eligible. These two processes are likely to be such that participants have unobservable (to the econometrician) characteristics that are systematically different from those of the non-participants. Fortunately, given the information at our disposal it is possible to devise estimators that, under very general assumptions, will yield unbiased estimates of the programs' impacts. These estimators are presented in the next section.

3. Modeling labour market transitions

The labour market history of a given individual is represented by a sequence of n spells of various lengths in any of K (=7) states[11]. Let x_t be the state in which an individual is observed to be at time t. The sequence starts at calendar time $\tau_0 = 0$ when the individual is 16 years of age and ends at time τ_e ($\tau_e =$ December 1993). Figure 3 depicts a hypothetical sequence made up of 3 spells of various length in 3 different states. As depicted, the individual is initially observed in the OLF state. He enters into employment at time τ_1 and eventually moves into unemployment at time τ_2. At time τ_e he is still in the midst of an unemployment spell.

Let τ_ℓ denote the calendar time at which a spell in any given state ends. Each spell ℓ ($1 \leq \ell \leq n$) is thus delimited by the start time $\tau_{\ell-1}$ and the end time τ_ℓ ($\tau_\ell > \tau_{\ell-1}$). Let u_ℓ be the duration of spell ℓ ($u_\ell = \tau_\ell - \tau_{\ell-1}$). Finally, let r denote a complete sequence from time 0 to time τ_e :

$$r = ((u_1, x_{\tau_1}), \ldots, (u_{n-1}, x_{\tau_{n-1}}), (u_n, 0)),$$

where $u_n = \tau_e - \tau_{n-1}$ is the duration of the last spell. The last spell of each individual is right-censored since τ_n and x_{τ_n} are not observed. On the other hand, the last spell must have lasted at least $\tau_n - \tau_{n-1}$ units of time in state $x_{\tau_{n-1}}$. Because x_{τ_n} is not observed we conventionally fix $x_{\tau_n} = 0$.

[11] See Fougère & Kamionka (2008) for a more general presentation of the econometrics of transition models.

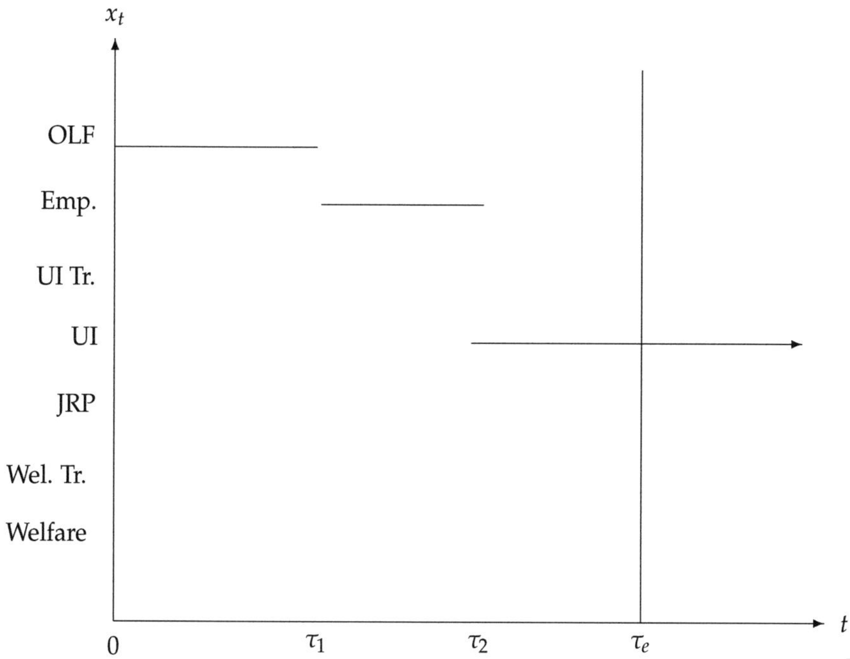

Fig. 3. Labour market history of a hypothetical individual.

The sequence may be more compactly rewritten as:

$$r = (y_1, \ldots, y_n),$$

where

$$y_\ell = \begin{cases} (u_\ell, x_{\tau_\ell}), & \text{if } 1 \leq \ell \leq n-1, \\ (u_n, 0), & \text{if } \ell = n. \end{cases}$$

The initial state, x_0, is the same for each individual in our sample and is exogenously determined by school attendance laws. Consequently, there is no need to explicitly model the initial state in which individuals are observed.

3.1 Likelihood function

Each individual contributes a sequence $r = (y_1, \ldots, y_n)$ to the likelihood function. The contribution can be written conditionally on a vector of exogenous variables, z, and an unobserved heterogeneity factor, v.

Let $l_v(\theta)$ denote the conditional contribution of the sequence r. We have,

$$l_v(\theta) = \prod_{\ell=1}^{n} f(y_\ell \mid y_1, \ldots, y_{\ell-1}; z; v; \theta),$$

where $f(y_\ell \mid y_1, \ldots, y_{\ell-1}; z; v; \theta)$ is the conditional density of y_ℓ given y_1, ..., $y_{\ell-1}$, z and v, and $\theta \in \Theta \subset \mathbb{R}^p$ is a vector of parameters. Naturally, the destination state of the last spell is unknown since the duration is censored. Its contribution to the conditional likelihood function is limited to the survivor function of the observed duration.

The random variable v is assumed to be independently and identically distributed across individuals, and independent from the exogenous variables z. If the unobserved heterogeneity can take only a finite number of values, $v_1, \ldots, v_J$, the contribution of a sequence r to the likelihood function is

$$l(\theta) = \sum_{j=1}^{J} \prod_{\ell=1}^{n} f(y_\ell \mid y_1, \ldots, y_{\ell-1}; z; v_j; \theta)\, \pi_j, \tag{1}$$

where π_j is the probability that the unobserved heterogeneity term takes the value v_j ($0 \leq \pi_j \leq 1, \sum_{j=1}^{J} \pi_j = 1$).

If v is a continuous random variable, then

$$l(\theta) = \int_V \prod_{\ell=1}^{n} f(y_\ell \mid y_1, \ldots, y_{\ell-1}; z; v; \theta)\, g(v; \gamma)\, dv, \tag{2}$$

where $g(v;\gamma)$ is a density probability function and V is the support of v.

Furthermore, if we assume that Y_ℓ is independent of $Y_1, \ldots, Y_{\ell-2}$, given $Y_{\ell-1} = y_{\ell-1}$, $Z = z$ and the value of the unobserved term v, then

$$f(y_\ell \mid y_1, \ldots, y_{\ell-1}; z; v; \theta) = f(y_\ell \mid y_{\ell-1}; z; v; \theta).$$

Given the history of the process, the joint distribution of the duration of spell ℓ and the destination state only depends on the current state on the labour market. This assumption will be relaxed by introducing other characteristics of the history of the process.

3.2 Modeling individual spells

In this section we focus on the conditional distribution of $y_\ell = (u_\ell, x_{\tau_\ell})$, where u_ℓ is the duration of the ℓth spell in state $x_{\tau_{\ell-1}}$. Define $u^*_{\ell,k}$ as the waiting time before leaving state $x_{\tau_{\ell-1}}$ for state x_{τ_ℓ}. At the end of the ℓth spell, the individual will enter into the state corresponding to the smallest latent duration $u^*_{\ell,k'}$. We will assume that these K latent durations are independently distributed. Thus the duration of spell ℓ is given by[12]

$$u_\ell = \inf_{k'} u^*_{\ell,k'}.$$

Let $f_j(u \mid y_1, \ldots, y_{\ell-1}; z; v; \theta)$ denote the probability density function (p.d.f.) of the latent duration $u^*_{\ell,j}$, given the history of the process up to time $\tau_{\ell-1}$, v and covariates z. Let $S_j(u \mid y_1, \ldots, y_{\ell-1}; z; v; \theta)$ be the corresponding survivor function:

$$S_j(u \mid y_1, \ldots, y_{\ell-1}; z; v; \theta) = \int_u^{+\infty} f_j(s \mid y_1, \ldots, y_{\ell-1}; z; v; \theta)\, ds.$$

[12] If the transition from state i to state j cannot be observed, we assume that the corresponding latent distribution is defective and set a probability mass equal to one on $+\infty$.

The conditional joint density of the duration of spell ℓ and the destination state k is given by the following expression

$$f(u,k|y_1,\dots,y_{\ell-1};z;v;\theta) = f_k(u \mid y_1,\dots,y_{\ell-1};z;v;\theta) \prod_{\substack{j=1 \\ j\neq k}}^{K} S_j(u \mid y_1,\dots,y_{\ell-1};z;v;\theta),$$

$$= h_k(u|y_1,\dots,y_{\ell-1};z;v;\theta)\, S(u|y_1,\dots,y_{\ell-1};z;v;\theta),$$

where $h_k(u \mid y_1,\dots,y_{\ell-1};z;v;\theta)$ is the hazard function associated with the latent duration $u^*_{\ell,k}$ and $S(u \mid y_1,\dots,y_{\ell-1};z;v;\theta)$ is the survivor function of the duration of the ℓth spell. Because the latent durations are assumed to be conditionally independent we have

$$S(u \mid y_1,\dots,y_{\ell-1};z;v;\theta) = \prod_{j=1}^{K} S_j(u \mid y_1,\dots,y_{\ell-1};z;v;\theta),$$

where $u \geq 0$. The expression represents the conditional probability that the duration of spell ℓ is at least equal to u or, equivalently, that all latent durations are at least equal to u. Therefore, the conditional contribution of a given sequence to the likelihood function is:

$$l_v(\theta) = \prod_{\ell=1}^{n}\prod_{k=1}^{K} h_k(u \mid y_1,\dots,y_{\ell-1};z;v;\theta)^{\delta_{\ell,k}}\, S_k(u \mid y_1,\dots,y_{\ell-1};z;v;\theta),$$

where $\delta_{\ell,k}$ is equal to 1 if the individual enters into state k at the end of spell ℓ and to 0 otherwise :

$$\delta_{\ell,k} = \begin{cases} 1, & \text{if } x_{\tau_\ell} = k, \\ 0, & \text{otherwise,} \end{cases}$$

$\ell = 1,\dots,n.$

3.3 Unobserved heterogeneity

So far the discussion surrounding the unobserved heterogeneity components has voluntarily been kept general. The use of maximum likelihood procedures requires that we specify distribution functions for these components. Most applications rely on the work of Heckman & Singer (1984) and approximate arbitrary continuous distributions using a finite number of mass points (see Gritz (1993), Ham & Rea (1987), Doiron & Gorgens (2008)). More recent papers use richer specifications that allow the heterogeneity terms to be correlated across states (see Bonnal et al. (1997), Ham & LaLonde (1996)). These specifications are sometimes referred to as single or two-factor loading distributions and are also based on a finite set of mass points. In our work, we wish to investigate the robustness of the parameter estimates to various distributional assumptions. We will use two and three-factor loading distributions as in the aforementioned papers. Additionally, we will investigate the consequences on the slope parameters of using various continuous distributions instead of the usual finite sets of mass points.

To fix ideas, let $w = (w_1, \ldots, w_K)$ be a vector of unobserved heterogeneity variables, with w_k a destination-specific component ($k = 1, \ldots, K$). Ideally, the joint distribution of the unobserved heterogeneity terms should not be independent.
Consider first a two-factor loading model (see Van den Berg (1997)) such that

$$w_k = \exp(a_k\, v_1 + b_k\, v_2), \tag{3}$$

where $v_1 \in \{-2, c_2\}$, $v_2 \in \{c_1, c_2\}$, $b_k \in \mathbb{R}$, $a_k = \mathbf{1}[k \geq 2]$ and $b_1 = 1$. The random variables v_1 and v_2 are assumed to be independent. The constraints imposed on the support of v_1 and v_2 are sufficient for identification and to allow the correlation between $\log(w_k)$ and $\log(w_{k'})$ to span the interval $[-1; 1]$.
Moreover, assume that

$$\text{Prob}[(V_1, V_2) = (v_1^0, v_2^0)] = \begin{cases} p^2, & \text{if } v_1^0 = -2 \text{ and } v_2^0 = c_1, \\ p * (1-p), & \text{if } v_1^0 = -2 \text{ and } v_2^0 = c_2, \\ (1-p) * p, & \text{if } v_1^0 = c_2 \text{ and } v_2^0 = c_1, \\ (1-p)^2, & \text{if } v_1^0 = c_2 \text{ and } v_2^0 = c_2, \end{cases} \tag{4}$$

where $c_1, c_2 \in \mathbb{R}$ and the probability p is defined as

$$p = \frac{\exp(d)}{1 + \exp(d)},$$

where $d \in \mathbb{R}$ is a parameter.
The correlation between $\log(w_k)$ and $\log(w_{k'})$, denoted $\rho_{k,k'}$, is

$$\rho_{k,k'} = \frac{a_k\, a_{k'} \sigma_{v_1}^2 + b_k\, b_{k'}\, \sigma_{v_2}^2}{\sqrt{a_k^2\, \sigma_{v_1}^2 + b_k^2\, \sigma_{v_2}^2}\sqrt{a_{k'}^2\, \sigma_{v_1}^2 + b_{k'}^2\, \sigma_{v_2}^2}}, \tag{5}$$

where $k, k' = 1, \ldots, K$ and $\sigma_{v_j}^2$ is the variance of v_j, j=1,2. A positive correlation coefficient between w_j and w_k implies that those who are likely to have high transition rates between any given state and state j will also have high transition rates into state k.
A two-factor loading model with two independent heterogeneity terms with common continuous distribution can also be derived from this specification. As before, let w_k denote the heterogeneity term for destination k:

$$w_k = \exp(a_k\, v_1 + b_k\, v_2),$$

where a_k and b_k are parameters ($a_k = \mathbf{1}[k \geq 2]$ and $b_1 = 1$).
Here v_1 and v_2 are assumed to be independently and identically distributed. Let $q(v; \gamma)$ be the p.d.f. of v_1 and v_2. The correlations between $\log(w_k)$ and $\log(w_{k'})$ are given by the same expression as in (5). In principle, $q(v; \gamma)$ represents any well-behaved distribution function.
The above specification can be further generalized to a three-factor loading model with common continuous distribution. In this case the unobserved components depend on the destination state as well as the current state. Let $w_{j,k}$ be specific to the transition between origin j and destination k.

$$w_{j,k} = w_j'\, w_k = \exp(a_j'\, v_3 + b_j'\, v_2) \times \exp(a_k\, v_1 + b_k\, v_2), \tag{6}$$

where a_j', b_j', a_k and b_k are parameters ($a_j' = a_k = \mathbf{1}[k \geq 2]$, $b_1 = 1$).

In this three-factor loading model, the correlation between destination states k and k' is

$$\rho_{k,k'} = \frac{a_k\, a_{k'} + b_k\, b_{k'}}{\sqrt{a_k^2 + b_k^2}\sqrt{a_{k'}^2 + b_{k'}^2}}. \tag{7}$$

This correlation has the same interpretation as in the two-factor loading model.
On the other hand, the correlation between the two origin states j and j' is given by

$$\rho_{j,j'} = \frac{a'_j\, a'_{j'} + b'_j\, b'_{j'}}{\sqrt{a'^2_j + b'^2_j}\sqrt{a'^2_{j'} + b'^2_{j'}}}. \tag{8}$$

A positive correlation indicates that those who have short spells in state j are likely to have short spell duration in state j' as well.
Finally, the correlation between origin state j and destination state k is given by

$$\rho_{k,j} = \frac{b'_j\, b_k}{\sqrt{a'^2_j + b'^2_j}\sqrt{a_k^2 + b_k^2}}, \tag{9}$$

where $j, j', k, k' = 1, \ldots, K$. This correlation is somewhat trickier to interpret. A positive coefficient indicates that those who are likely to have short spell duration in state j are also more likely to enter state k. Conversely, those who are more likely to have short spell duration in state j are less likely to enter state k.

3.4 Specification of conditional hazard functions

Assume an individual is observed in state j during spell ℓ (i.e. $x_{\tau_{\ell-1}} = j$). Let $\psi(j,k)$ denote the heterogeneity term for destination k, given the individual is in state j. There are two possibilities:

$$\psi(j,k) = \begin{cases} w_k, & \text{in the two-factor loading model,} \\ w_{j,k}, & \text{in the three-factor loading model.} \end{cases}$$

The conditional hazard function for transition (j,k) is given by

$$h_{j,k}(u \mid y_1, \ldots, y_{\ell-1}; z; v; \theta) = h^0_{j,k}(u;\theta)\; \varphi(y_1, \ldots, y_{\ell-1}; z; \theta)\; \psi(j,k), \tag{10}$$

where φ is a positive function of the exogenous variables and the sequence r, $h^0_{j,k}(u;\theta)$ is the baseline hazard function for transition (j,k), and $\psi(j,k) > 0$.
We have considered three alternative conditional specifications for the baseline hazard functions. For each transition, we have chosen among the following competing specifications on the basis of non-parametric kernel estimations (see Fortin et al. (1999a)):

1. *Log-logistic Distribution*
   The baseline hazard function is

$$h^0_{j,k}(u;\theta) = \frac{\beta_{j,k}\, \alpha_{j,k}\, u^{\alpha_{j,k}-1}}{(1 + \beta_{j,k}\, u^{\alpha_{j,k}})},$$

$\alpha_{j,k}, \beta_{j,k} \in \mathbb{R}^+$.

If $\alpha_{j,k} > 1$ then the hazard function is increasing then decreasing with respect of u. If $\alpha_{j,k} \leq 1$ then the hazard function is decreasing.

2. *Piecewise-Constant Hazard Model*

   The expression of the baseline hazard function is

$$h^0_{j,k}(u;\theta) = \alpha_{j,k}\mathbf{1}[u < u^0_1] + \beta_{j,k}\mathbf{1}[u^0_1 \leq u < u^0_2] + \gamma_{j,k}\mathbf{1}[u^0_2 \leq u],$$

   where $\alpha_{j,k}, \beta_{j,k}, \gamma_{j,k} \in \mathbb{R}^+$. u^0_1 and u^0_2 are fixed.

   The baseline hazard function can be increasing then decreasing, decreasing then increasing, strictly increasing or strictly decreasing.

3. *Weibull Distribution*

   The baseline hazard function is

$$h^0_{j,k}(u;\theta) = \alpha_{j,k}\,\beta_{j,k}\,u^{\alpha_{j,k}-1},$$

   $\alpha_{j,k}, \beta_{j,k} \in \mathbb{R}^+$.

   If $\alpha_{j,k} > 1$ then the hazard function is increasing with respect of u. If $\alpha_{j,k} < 1$ then the hazard function is decreasing with respect of u and if $\alpha_{j,k} = 1$ this conditional hazard function is constant.

3.5 Estimation

We consider three alternative specifications for the unobserved heterogeneity distribution.

1. *Two-Factor Loading and Discrete Distribution*

   The log likelihood is

$$\log(L(\theta)) = \sum_{i=1}^{N} \log(l_i(\theta)), \tag{11}$$

   where $l_i(\theta)$ is obtained by substituting the sequence $r_i = (y_{1,i}, \ldots, y_{n_i,i})$ and the observed vector of covariates z_i in (1). N is the size of the sample.

   In equation (1) π_j is set equal to[13]

$$\pi_j = \begin{cases} p^2, & \text{if } j = 1, \\ p*(1-p), & \text{if } j = 2,3, \\ (1-p)^2, & \text{if } j = 4, \end{cases}$$

   where $p \in [0;1]$ is a parameter. The log-likelihood is then maximized with respect of θ $(\theta \in \Theta)$.

2. *Two-Factor Loading and Continuous Distribution*

   The model includes two unobserved heterogeneity terms v_1 and v_2 ($v_j > 0, j = 1,2$). We assume these terms to be independently and identically distributed. Let $q(v;\gamma)$ be the p.d.f. of v_j, $j = 1,2$.

   The contribution of a given realization to the likelihood function is given by equation (2), where $\nu = (v_1, v_2)'$, $V = \mathbb{R}^+ \times \mathbb{R}^+$ and $g(\nu;\gamma) = q(v_1;\gamma)\,q(v_2;\gamma)$. The log-likelihood is

[13] See section 4.

given by equation (11), where $l_i(\theta)$ is the contribution to the likelihood of the sequence r_i.[14] Since the integral in $l(\theta)$ cannot generally be analytically computed it must be numerically simulated.

Let $\hat{l}(\theta)$ denote the estimator of the individual contribution to the likelihood function. We assume that

$$\hat{l}(\theta) = \frac{1}{H}\sum_{h=1}^{H}\prod_{\ell=1}^{n} f(y_\ell \mid y_1, \ldots, y_{\ell-1}; z; v_{1,h}, v_{2,h}; \theta),$$

where $v_{1,h}$ and $v_{2,h}$ are drawn independently according to the p.d.f. $q(v;\gamma)$. The drawings $v_{j,h}$ ($j = 1, 2$, $h = 1, \ldots, H$) are assumed to be specific to the individual. The parameter estimates are obtained by maximizing the simulated log-likelihood:

$$\log(L(\theta)) = \sum_{i=1}^{N} \log(\hat{l}_i(\theta)),$$

where $\hat{l}_i(\theta)$ is the simulated contribution of the sequence r_i to the likelihood function.

The maximization of this simulated likelihood yields consistent and efficient parameters estimates if $\frac{\sqrt{N}}{H} \to 0$ when $H \to +\infty$ and $N \to +\infty$ (see Gourriéroux & Monfort (1991)). Under these conditions, this estimator has the same asymptotic distribution as the standard ML estimator. Following Laroque & Salanié (1993), Kamionka (1998) and Edon & Kamionka (2007) we have used 20 draws from the random distributions when estimating the models. Using as few as 10 draws yielded essentially the same parameter estimates.

3. *Three-Factor Loading and Continuous Distribution*

In the three-factor loading model the conditional contribution must be integrated with respect to the distribution of three independent unobserved heterogeneity terms. Let $\hat{l}(\theta)$ denote the estimator of the individual contribution to the likelihood function. Assume further that

$$\hat{l}(\theta) = \frac{1}{H}\sum_{h=1}^{H}\prod_{\ell=1}^{n} f(y_\ell \mid y_1, \ldots, y_{\ell-1}; z; v_{1,h}, v_{2,h}, v_{3,h}; \theta),$$

where $v_{1,h}$, $v_{2,h}$ and $v_{3,h}$ are drawn independently according to the p.d.f. $q(v;\gamma)$. Once again, the parameter estimates obtained from maximizing this function are asymptotically efficient.

4. Estimation results

This section presents the results of fitting the models outlined in the previous section to the data at our disposal. The estimation of such complex models is computationally demanding. Also, a number of issues must be addressed before dwelling into the results.

4.1 Functional forms assumptions

As mentioned in the previous section, it is necessary to specify a baseline distribution function for each transition considered in the model. When selecting a particular functional form, a

[14] In what follows, θ includes γ, the parameters of $q(\cdot)$.

number of desirable properties should be sought. First, the functional form should allow a number of different shapes of the hazard function so that various combinations of positive and negative duration dependence are possible. Second, it should roughly follow the pattern of transitions times found in the data. Finally, the functional forms should involve as few parameters as possible.

Dest. / *Origin*	Welfare	Welfare Training	JRP	U.I.	U.I. Training	Emp.	OLF
Welfare		Exp (1)	Exp (1)	Exp (1)		Exp (3)	Exp (1)
Wel Tr	Log-logis.					Log-logis.	Log-logis.
JRP						Exp (1)	
U.I.	Exp (2)		Exp (2)	Exp (1)	Exp (3)	Exp (2)	
U.I. Tr						Exp (1)	
Emp	Log-logis.	Weibull	Log-logis.		Log-logis.	Log-logis.	
OLF	Exp (2)	Exp (2)	Exp (2)		Exp (2)		

Table 3. Baseline Hazard Functional Forms†

† "Exp" refers to exponential piecewise constant hazard model. The number of parameters are indicated between parentheses.

The data at our disposal was analyzed in Fortin et al. (1999a) and Fortin et al. (2004) using non-parametric kernel hazard estimators. The baseline hazard functions were chosen on the basis of their analysis. Table 3 reports the functional form used in each of the 24 transitions considered in the model. Both the log-logistic and the piecewise constant functions allow non-monotonic hazards. For many transitions, the empirical hazard functions initially increase for a short period of time and then display an extended period of negative duration dependence. The log-logistic function is best suited in these cases. When the empirical hazard function looks relatively flat, it is preferable to use an exponential model with a single parameter. Other non-monotone shapes are best approximated with the piecewise constant hazard function. Monotone increasing or decreasing empirical hazard rates can be satisfactorily approximated with a weibull distribution function.

4.2 Exogenous covariates

Most studies on labour market transitions include a number of exogenous individual-specific and macroeconomic variables. It is thus customary to include variables such as age, sex, education and minority status to capture behavioural differences across these groups. In this chapter we have tried to limit the number of exogenous control variables as much as possible. Given the unusually large number of transitions considered in the analysis, including even as little as 10 exogenous variables would have over-parameterized the likelihood function and rendered its estimation practically infeasible.

An alternative empirical strategy is to circumscribe the sample to relatively homogeneous individuals in terms of observable characteristics. We have elected to concentrate our attention on young and poorly educated men for two reasons: (1) They have fared relatively poorly on the labour market over the past two decades (see Beaudry & Green (2000)); (2) As a consequence of their deteriorating labour market outcomes, many have claimed welfare benefits and have been especially targeted for training programs. Having a relatively homogeneous sample in terms of age and education does not remove the need to control for such variables explicitly. Our sampling scheme insures that there is little variance in age at the start of the sample period (see Table 1). As the initial individuals become older, new entrants 18–19 years of age join the sample, thus increasing considerably the variance in age. On the other hand, the sample was chosen so that educational attainment never exceeded 10 years of schooling. Consequently, the variance in education remains relatively constant over the sample period.

We thus explicitly control for age in the regressions. Note that Gritz (1993) has found both education and age to have little impact on any of the transitions considered in his model. The following exogenous variables are included in the model in addition to age: minimum wage, unemployment rate, welfare benefits, and dummy indicators for previous training under either welfare or UI. The minimum wage and the welfare benefits are computed monthly and deflated by the monthly Consumer Price Index (CPI). The monthly unemployment rate is computed for men aged 25-64 for the Province of Québec. All the variables are computed at the beginning of each spell and are assumed constant throughout the duration of individual spells.

4.3 Parameter estimates

Table 4 presents the parameter estimates of a three-factor loading model that incorporates a weibull distribution for the heterogeneity variables.[15] The slope parameters of the non-parametric and the (weibull) two-factor loading models are nearly identical to those presented in Table 4 and are not reported for the sake of brevity.

Table 4 is divided into several panels. Each panel contains the parameter estimates for the exit rates of a given state. The parameter estimates of the baseline hazard are presented first followed by those of the control variables. The variable "Wel Tr_1" is a dummy indicator that equals 1 if the individual has experienced a welfare training spell or has participated in JRP at any time prior to the ongoing spell, and 0 otherwise. The variable "Wel Tr_2" is a dummy indicator that equals 1 if the state just prior to the current spell was either welfare training or JRP, and 0 otherwise. The variables "UI Tr_1" and "UI Tr_2" are similarly defined but pertain to UI training programs. The inclusion of "Wel $Tr1_1$" or "UI Tr_1" alone implicitly assumes that the impact of training programs does not wear off with time nor that it accumulate with repeat uses. Including both "Wel Tr_1" and "Wel Tr_2" or "UI Tr_1" and "UI Tr_2" allows to determine whether recent training has more impact than previous training on current spell duration. Both past and recent training variables are included whenever feasible.

4.3.1 Exits from welfare

The first panel of Table 4 focuses on exits from welfare. Exits to as many as five different states are considered in the model. Parameters related to age indicate that as individuals get older they are more likely to enter employment or OLF upon leaving welfare. In the latter case, this may be an indication that they are more inclined to return to school. Increases in the minimum wage rate increases the transitions towards welfare training, JRP and unemployment, but has no impact on transitions into employment. This result is compatible with the results found

[15] The model was also estimated using normal, student-t, χ^2 and gamma distributions. The results based on these specifications are not reported here for the sake of brevity, but are available on request. The specification based on the weibull was preferred to all others for two reasons. First, the parameter estimates based on the weibull distribution are very similar to those based on discrete distributions with a finite number of mass points. Given the latter are robust to specification errors on the distribution of the heterogeneity components (see Heckman & Singer (1984)), the weibull distribution appears to depict similar properties. Second, as in Heckman & Singer (1984), the value of likelihood function based on the weibull distribution is larger than those based on other distributions.

	No Het	Non-Para	Log-Normal	Weibull 2 Factors	Weibull 2 Factors	Weibull 3 Factors
Welfare to Welfare Training						
Baseline[1]	12.951†	11.769†	9.916†	9.736†	7.437†	7.511†
Replacement	-41.844†	-34.680†	-34.591†	-34.500†	-30.710†	-30.722†
Minimum Wage	11.507†	10.464†	10.555†	10.624†	10.132†	10.127†
Unemp Rate	1.837†	0.641†	0.659†	0.659†	0.855†	0.858†
Welfare Ben.	-0.267	-1.202†	-1.165†	-1.169†	-1.058†	-1.046†
Wel. Tr.[3]					0.133	0.126
JRP[4]					0.486†	0.486†
U.I. Tr.[5]					0.123	0.127
Welfare to JRP						
Baseline[1]	-16.915‡	-12.068	-20.602†	-21.019†	23.330†	-23.004†
Replacement	-2.948	10.486	11.451	11.010	14.679	14.800
Minimum Wage	24.425†	20.061†	20.504†	20.511†	20.177†	19.689†
Unemp Rate	0.114	-2.402†	-2.477†	-2.465†	-2.301†	-2.304†
Welfare Ben.	1.389	0.081	0.093	0.046	0.115	0.095
Wel. Tr.[3]					0.562‡	0.561‡
JRP[4]					-0.011	-0.039
U.I. Tr.[5]					0.112	0.109
Welfare to Unemployment						
Baseline[1]	2.275	0.160	-5.840	-6.134	-3.910	-3.511
Replacement	-30.577†	-16.447	-15.796	-16.035	-19.417‡	-18.808‡
Minimum Wage	12.777	16.201†	16.575†	16.565†	16.483†	15.791†
Unemp Rate	1.538†	-0.399	-0.446	-0.451	-0.568	-0.547
Welfare Ben.	1.579‡	0.672	0.682	0.626	0.571	0.456
Wel. Tr.[3]					0.232	0.210
JRP[4]					-2.164‡	-2.139‡
U.I. Tr.[5]					0.594	0.531
Welfare to Work						
Baseline[2]	-6.268†	5.172†	-1.084	-1.426	-0.781	-0.902
	-6.786†	4.757†	-1.501	-1.836	-1.194	-1.250
	-7.623†	4.039†	-2.253	-2.580	-1.941	-1.910
Replacement	-0.201	-2.715	-2.268	-2.469	-3.464	-2.834
Minimum Wage	6.019†	-0.608	-0.470	-0.447	-0.345	-0.266
Unemp Rate	-0.322†	-0.106	-0.127	-0.126	-0.209	-0.219
Welfare Ben.	-1.107†	-1.214†	-1.204†	-1.231†	-1.272†	-1.342†
Wel. Tr.[3]					0.027	0.020
JRP[4]					-0.454†	-0.436†
U.I. Tr.[5]					0.314	0.273
Welfare to OLF						
Baseline[1]	-2.676	-1.632	-1.661	-1.858	-1.136	-1.025
Replacement	-3.865	-6.066‡	-6.159‡	-5.847	-6.859‡	-6.669‡
Minimum Wage	-1.026	-1.394	-1.424	-1.268	-1.130	-1.055
Unemp Rate	0.396†	0.500†	0.484†	0.508†	0.382	0.425‡
Welfare Ben.	-0.847†	-0.621†	-0.522†	-0.590†	-0.632†	-0.684†
Wel. Tr.[3]					-0.209	-0.242
JRP[4]					-0.276	-0.233
U.I. Tr.[5]					0.708†	0.597†

Table 4. Parameter Estimates – Exits from Welfare

[1] *Exponential hazard.*
[2] *Exponential hazard – splines.*
[3] *Dummy indicator for any previous welfare training.*
[4] *Dummy indicator for any previous JRP.*
[5] *Dummy indicator for any previous U.I. training.*

	No Het	Non-Para	Log-Normal	Weibull 2 Factors	Weibull 2 Factors	Weibull 3 Factors
Unemployment to Welfare						
Baseline[2]	-20.617†	-28.243†	-29.821†	-29.848†	-29.184†	-29.120†
	-17.591†	-25.197†	-26.775†	-26.805†	-26.039†	-25.969†
Replacement	22.900†	31.891†	31.726†	31.632†	31.541†	31.616†
Minimum Wage	-5.551	5.312†	5.125†	5.129†	3.266	3.236
Unemp Rate	1.695†	0.907‡	0.921‡	0.921‡	1.084†	1.093†
Welfare Ben.	1.620†	1.289†	1.313†	1.314†	1.403†	1.401†
Wel. Tr.[3]					0.590†	0.583†
JRP[4]					-0.045	-0.046
U.I. Tr.[5]					2.161†	2.171†
Unemployment to Unemployment						
Baseline[2]	-20.463†	-1.743	-7.615	-7.912	-7.524	-7.390
	-16.030†	2.695	-3.168	-3.473	-3.016	-2.884
Replacement	3.966	-1.913	-1.024	-1.382	-1.547	-1.442
Minimum Wage	22.232†	1.669	1.197	1.309	0.371	0.192
Unemp Rate	0.901†	0.947‡	0.981‡	0.973‡	1.042‡	1.065‡
Welfare Ben.	-1.245†	-1.235†	-1.179†	-1.203†	-1.161†	-1.153†
Wel. Tr.[3]					0.315	0.338
JRP[4]					0.305	0.301
U.I. Tr.[5]					1.477†	1.473†
Unemployment to Unemployment Training						
Baseline[1]	-2.325	-6.534	-10.807	-10.988	-10.621	-10.482
Replacement	-15.630‡	-4.039	-4.201	-4.171	-5.389	-5.474
Minimum Wage	4.588	11.050†	11.140†	11.207†	11.962†	11.915†
Unemp Rate	1.758	0.329	0.311	0.299	0.202	0.210
Welfare Ben.	0.934	0.160	0.192	0.203	0.190	0.203
Wel. Tr.[3]					-0.398	-0.408
U.I. Tr.[5]					-0.144	-0.146
Unemployment to Work						
Baseline[2]	-5.570‡	10.517†	4.550‡	3.985	4.577‡	4.730‡
	-3.400	12.708†	6.753†	6.181†	6.788†	6.938†
Replacement	-3.153	-10.825†	-10.570†	-10.526†	-11.610†	-11.669†
Minimum Wage	8.237†	-3.261†	-3.719†	-3.532†	-3.364†	-3.478†
Unemp Rate	-0.801†	-0.266	-0.225	-0.235	-0.277	-0.269
Welfare Ben.	-0.683†	-0.337	-0.299	-0.326	-0.342	-0.330
Wel. Tr.[3]					-0.385†	-0.368†
JRP [4]					0.150	0.156
U.I. Tr.[5]					0.774†	0.784†
Unemployment to OLF						
Baseline[2]	-13.698†	-10.051†	-9.952†	-10.042†	-9.426†	-9.302†
	-10.723†	-7.069†	-6.986†	-7.079†	-6.418†	-6.293†
Replacement	7.977†	6.497‡	6.104‡	6.375‡	5.533	5.353
Minimum Wage	8.652†	2.008	2.358	2.402	2.015	1.984
Unemp Rate	-0.054	-0.236	-0.295	-0.305	-0.271	-0.252
Welfare Ben.	-0.284	-0.390	-0.406	-0.396	-0.378	-0.361
Wel. Tr.					-0.098	-0.127
JRP					0.045	0.061
U.I. Tr.					1.399†	1.353†

Table 4. Continued: Parameter Estimates – Exits from Unemployment

[1] *Exponential hazard.*
[2] *Exponential hazard – splines.*
[3] *Dummy indicator for any previous welfare training.*
[4] *Dummy indicator for any previous JRP.*
[5] *Dummy indicator for any previous U.I. training.*

	No Het	Non-Para	Log-Normal	Weibull 2 Factors	Weibull 2 Factors	Weibull 3 Factors
Work to Welfare						
Baseline[1]	-7.102†	-7.122†	-7.093†	-7.094†	-7.066†	-7.057†
	1.825†	1.829†	1.823†	1.823†	1.815†	1.812†
Replacement	-10.487†	-7.783†	-10.196†	-10.328†	-10.415†	-10.336†
Minimum Wage	0.165	1.045	0.230	0.207	0.172	0.175
Unemp Rate	1.022†	0.939†	1.002†	1.008†	1.083†	1.087†
Welfare Ben.	1.078†	0.977†	1.050†	1.050†	1.026†	1.038†
Wel. Tr.[2]					0.698†	0.692†
JRP[3]					-1.167†	-1.166†
U.I. Tr.[4]					-0.313	-0.306
Work to Welfare Training						
Baseline[1]	-29.322†	7.320	5.564	5.571	2.880	3.647
	3.352†	-0.012	-0.019	-0.020	-0.004	-0.006
Replacement	-35.936†	-43.508†	-43.520†	-43.638†	-34.009†	-35.355†
Minimum Wage	25.433†	26.226†	26.392†	26.342†	18.898†	18.242†
Unemp Rate	-0.107	-0.610	-0.623	-0.614	-0.282	-0.161
Welfare Ben.	-1.249†	-1.389‡	-1.380‡	-1.374‡	-0.818	-0.629
Wel. Tr.[2]					1.281†	1.267†
JRP[3]					0.510†	0.500†
U.I. Tr.[4]					-1.067‡	-0.996
Work to Unemployment						
Baseline[1]	-6.340†	-6.453†	-6.492†	-6.468†	-6.474†	-6.445†
	0.687†	0.678†	0.671†	0.671†	0.673†	0.672†
Replacement	-2.411†	7.297†	-0.444	-1.208†	-1.309†	-1.171†
Minimum Wage	3.196†	5.624†	3.772†	3.612†	3.734†	3.757†
Unemp Rate	-0.805†	-0.959†	-0.934†	-0.896†	-0.898†	-0.910†
Welfare Ben.	-0.086	-0.436†	-0.228	-0.251	-0.265‡	-0.261‡
Wel. Tr1[2]					0.101	0.111
Wel. Tr2[5]					-0.216	-0.214
U.I. Tr1[3]					-0.130	-0.125
U.I. Tr2[6]					1.524†	1.484†
Work to Work						
Baseline[1]	-4.758†	-4.722†	-4.683†	-4.687†	-4.698†	-4.713†
	1.187†	1.155†	1.136†	1.143†	1.147†	1.162†
Replacement	-0.583	9.910†	1.320†	0.557	0.094	0.123
Minimum Wage	-3.339†	-1.263‡	-2.959†	-3.021†	-2.452†	-2.467†
Unemp Rate	-0.953†	-1.019†	-1.046†	-1.036†	-1.030†	-1.036†
Welfare Ben.	0.013	-0.285‡	-0.122	-0.142	-0.180	-0.159
Wel. Tr1[2]					-0.248	-0.240
Wel. Tr2[5]					-0.122	-0.123
U.I. Tr1[3]					0.014	0.027
U.I. Tr2[6]					-0.667	-0.716
Work to OLF						
Baseline[1]	-6.350‡	-6.283†	-6.332†	-6.336†	-6.356†	-6.310†
	1.650†	1.626†	1.641†	1.642†	1.645†	1.628†
Replacement	-0.060	-0.267	-0.480‡	-0.319	-1.205†	-1.246†
Minimum Wage	-3.623†	-3.903†	-3.774†	-3.811†	-2.606†	-2.717†
Unemp Rate	-0.974†	-0.916†	-0.911†	-0.908†	-0.915†	-0.877†
Welfare Ben.	0.268†	0.321†	0.317†	0.333†	0.260†	0.295†
Wel. Tr1[2]					-0.282†	-0.286†
Wel. Tr2[5]					-0.572†	-0.586†
U.I. Tr1[3]					-0.488†	-0.453†
U.I. Tr2[6]					-1.233	-1.237

Table 4. (Continued)Parameter Estimates – Exits from Employment

[1] *Log-logistic.*
[2] *Dummy indicator for any previous welfare training.*
[3] *Dummy indicator for any previous JRP.*
[4] *Dummy indicator for any previous U.I. training.*
[5] *Dummy indicator for prior state: welfare training.*
[6] *Dummy indicator for prior state: U.I. training.*

	No Het	Non-Para	Log-Normal	Weibull 2 Factors	Weibull 2 Factors	Weibull 3 Factors
OLF to Welfare						
Baseline[2]	9.050†	-21.852†	-23.272†	-23.247†	-21.271†	-21.201†
	8.014†	-22.698†	-24.168†	-24.150†	-22.170†	-22.082†
Replacement	-6.865†	24.985†	24.469†	24.301†	21.054†	21.196†
Minimum Wage	-22.989†	10.913†	10.664†	10.630†	10.589†	10.576†
Unemp Rate	0.384†	-0.425†	-0.378†	-0.376†	-0.386†	-0.396†
Welfare Ben.	1.759†	-0.002	0.039	0.049	0.038	0.032
Wel. Tr.[3]					0.261†	0.251†
JRP[4]					-1.236†	-1.229†
U.I. Tr.[5]					0.106	0.101
OLF to Welfare Training						
Baseline[2]	17.926†	-6.003†	-10.899†	-10.984†	-8.832†	-8.868†
	16.876†	-6.818†	-11.706†	-11.791†	-9.634†	-9.662†
Replacement	-64.337†	-29.309†	-25.939†	-25.960†	-25.370†	-26.066†
Minimum Wage	23.722†	34.225†	36.886†	36.923†	30.886†	31.237†
Unemp Rate	1.865†	0.547	0.351	0.341	0.940	0.961
Welfare Ben.	1.757†	-1.772‡	-1.824†	-1.819†	-1.769‡	-1.681‡
Wel. Tr.[3]					0.710†	0.711†
JRP[4]					-0.036	-0.087
U.I. Tr.[5]					0.105	0.201
OLF to Unemployment						
Baseline[2]	17.926†	-6.003†	-10.899†	-10.984†	-8.832†	-8.868†
	16.876†	-6.818†	-11.706†	-11.791†	-9.634†	-9.662†
Replacement	-18.873†	10.249†	9.571†	8.979†	4.909	5.430
Minimum Wage	-24.418†	8.757†	8.562†	8.549†	9.187†	9.175†
Unemp Rate	-1.791†	-2.838†	-2.892†	-2.919†	-2.926†	-2.984†
Welfare Ben.	1.047†	-0.309	-0.321	-0.326	-0.351	-0.359
Wel. Tr.[3]					-0.913†	-0.906†
JRP[4]					-0.046	-0.043
U.I. Tr.[5]					-0.380	-0.375
OLF to Work						
Baseline[2]	11.804†	-2.367	-8.492†	-8.596†	-6.903†	-6.977†
	11.148†	-2.701‡	-8.830†	-8.923†	-7.233†	-7.313†
Replacement	-6.325†	12.069†	12.465†	11.915†	9.093†	9.477†
Minimum Wage	-22.641†	3.718†	3.725†	3.742†	3.719†	3.664†
Unemp Rate	-1.950†	-2.861†	-2.896†	-2.934†	-2.938†	-2.957†
Welfare Ben.	0.098	-0.554†	-0.587†	-0.593†	-0.596†	-0.585†
Wel. Tr.[3]					-0.008	-0.007
JRP[4]					-0.612†	-0.618†
U.I. Tr.[5]					0.130	0.151

Table 4. (Continued)Parameter Estimates – Exits from OLF

[1] *Exponential hazard.*
[2] *Exponential hazard – splines.*
[3] *Dummy indicator for any previous welfare training.*
[4] *Dummy indicator for any previous JRP.*
[5] *Dummy indicator for any previous U.I. training.*

	No Het	Non-Para	Log-Normal	Weibull 2 Factors	Weibull 2 Factors	Weibull 3 Factors
Welfare Training to Welfare						
Baseline[1]	-4.927†	-4.997†	-4.951†	-4.949†	-4.950†	-5.036†
	0.508†	0.504†	0.506†	0.506†	0.506†	0.498†
Replacement	14.105†	16.989†	14.470†	14.324†	14.326†	15.040†
Minimum Wage	-16.050†	-14.842	-15.840†	-15.877†	-15.893†	-15.543†
Unemp Rate	-0.892†	-1.027†	-0.939†	-0.923†	-0.917†	-0.989†
Welfare Ben.	0.325	0.131	0.287	0.277	0.277	0.158
Welfare Training to Work						
Baseline[1]	-3.971†	-4.087†	-4.107†	-4.127†	-4.123†	-4.230†
	0.277†	0.277†	0.270†	0.268†	0.268†	0.262†
Replacement	-3.450†	5.666†	-1.437	-1.959	-2.100	-1.484
Minimum Wage	3.294†	7.772†	3.949‡	3.702‡	3.769‡	3.901‡
Unemp Rate	-0.957†	-1.096†	-0.884‡	-0.864‡	-0.857‡	-0.814
Welfare Ben.	-0.619	-1.233†	-1.019‡	-1.063‡	-1.060‡	-1.234†
Welfare Training to OLF						
Baseline[1]	-5.187†	-5.135†	-5.140†	-5.124†	-5.124†	-5.151†
	0.403†	0.405†	0.401†	0.403†	0.403†	0.404†
Replacement	-16.086†	-16.959†	-16.775†	-16.747†	-16.672†	-16.234†
Minimum Wage	14.358†	14.417†	13.960†	13.989†	13.957†	14.333†
Unemp Rate	-0.483	-0.515	-0.430	-0.430	-0.439	-0.486
Welfare Ben.	-0.219	-0.012	-0.014	0.024	0.021	-0.108
JRP to Work						
Baseline[2]	3.612	5.668	-3.143	-2.889	-3.037	-4.420
Replacement	-14.331†	-8.461	-5.173	-5.844	-5.767	-5.134
Minimum Wage	6.240	9.809	11.792	11.488	11.655	11.941‡
Unemp Rate	-0.276	-0.877	-1.024	-1.035	-1.047	-1.104
Welfare Ben.	-0.581	-1.467	-1.438	-1.731	-1.731	-0.670
Unemployment Training to Unemployment						
Baseline[2]	5.363	7.502†	1.457	0.920	1.233	0.822
Minimum Wage	-20.820†	-11.370†	-9.906†	-9.984†	-10.577†	-10.712†
Unemp Rate	0.480	1.571‡	1.452	1.525	1.559	1.544
Welfare Ben.	-0.084	0.369	0.157	0.231	0.213	0.506

Table 4. (Continued) Parameter Estimates – Exits from Training

[1] *Log-logistic.*

[2] *Exponential hazard.*

in a recent paper by Fortin et al. (2004). In that paper it was found using a similar sample that increases in the minimum wage rate increased exits from welfare. Since the transition state was not known, this was interpreted as evidence that firms were not constrained by the minimum wage rate. Instead, an increase in the latter was interpreted as attracting a number of welfare claimants onto the labour market. The results reported here provide a completely different story. Indeed, it appears that increases in the minimum wage rate induce welfare claimants to increase their employability status but does not translate into a larger number being employed. Quite to the contrary, the increased transition rates from welfare to unemployment suggest that a number of individuals who were working while claiming welfare benefits may have lost their job following the increase in the minimum wage rate.

Increases in the unemployment rate translate into smaller transition rates into JRP. This result is compatible with the fact that welfare claimants may be less motivated to increase their employability when job prospects diminish. Alternatively, firms may also be less inclined to hire trainees under the JRP program when the unemployment rate rise.

As expected, increases in welfare benefits decrease the exit rates from welfare. The result is statistically significant in transitions towards training, work and OLF states. A similar finding was reported by Fortin and Lacroix in the aforementioned paper.

Past occurrences of welfare training are generally not very beneficial to the men in our sample. They are associated with higher transition rates into welfare training and lower rates into employment and OLF. The impact is larger for recent occurrences, which suggests that participation in such training programs may convey a bad signal to potential employers. On the other hand, past occurrences of UI training has little impact on the exits from welfare.

4.3.2 Exits from unemployment

The next panel of the table focuses on the transitions from unemployment. Most parameter estimates that are statistically significant have the expected sign *a priori*. For instance, it is found that as individuals get older they are more likely to exit unemployment for employment and less for welfare. Similarly, increases in the minimum wage rate leads to higher transition rates into UI training but lower rates into employment. These results are consistent with those found with respect to exits from welfare.

Other results presented in the panel indicate that unemployed individuals are more likely to experience a new unemployment spell or to enter welfare and are less likely to enter employment whenever the unemployment rate increases. Presumably, a number of UI claimants can not find employment and therefore exhaust their benefits. The social security system in Canada entitles them to welfare benefits upon exhaustion of UI benefits. On the other hand, increases in welfare benefits increase the transition rates into welfare and lower those into unemployment and employment. These results suggest that the transitions towards employment are very sensitive to both policy variables, *i.e.* welfare benefits and minimum wages, as well as to the state of the economy as proxied by the unemployment rate.

A number of parameter estimates relating to the training dummy variables are statistically significant. Once again, previous participation in welfare training increases the likelihood of entering welfare upon leaving unemployment and decreases that of entering employment. On the other hand, recent UI training participation appears to have a conflicting impacts. Indeed, UI claimants are more likely to enter either welfare or UI upon leaving unemployment but are also more likely to enter employment. On the whole, these results are consistent with those found by Fortin et al. (1999b) using different data and econometric estimators and are also consistent to some extent with those of Gritz (1993) and Bonnal et al. (1997). In all three cases it was found that participation in government-sponsored training programs had detrimental effects on the labour market experience of young men. It has been suggested that potential employers may stigmatize participation in such training programs. Because these programs are designed to improve the labour market opportunities of disadvantaged workers, participation in the later may be taken as a signal of unsatisfactory performance in previous employment. Our results indicate that training while on welfare is detrimental to men, but training while on unemployment does not convey the same negative signal.

4.3.3 Exits from employment

The next panel of the table reports results relating to transitions from employment. Once again, most parameters estimates that are statistically significant have the expected sign. In particular, increases in the minimum wage rate is found to increase the likelihood of leaving employment for either welfare training, and to diminish considerably the likelihood of

entering a new job or moving into welfare. Increases in welfare benefits are found to increase the transitions into welfare and to decrease the likelihood of entering welfare training.
The parameter estimates associated with the unemployment rate has the expected sign except perhaps with respect to transitions between employment and unemployment. Indeed, the parameter estimate implies that whenever the unemployment rate increases, workers are less likely to leave employment to enter unemployment. There are several potential explanations for this result. First, it may well be that when the labour market deteriorates, workers who loose their job have difficulty qualify for UI benefits. Recall from Table 1 that the unconditional mean job duration is approximately 18 weeks, which is roughly equal to the qualifying period. They are thus more likely to turn to welfare, as indicated in the first column of the panel. Second, the deterioration of the labour market may induce some to hold on to their current job longer. The fact that all the parameter estimates are negative, except for welfare, is consistent with this possibility. Finally, increases in welfare benefits increase the transitions from employment to welfare, as expected.
The training variables show interesting results. For instance, those who have participated in welfare training are more likely to enter either welfare or welfare training upon exiting employment, although recent participation makes them less likely to enter welfare anew. Likewise, participation in welfare training translates into less employment–employment transitions. Those who were in UI training just prior to their current employment spell are much more likely to return to UI upon leaving employment and much less likely to experience an employment-employment transition. The likelihood of entering the OLF state following employment decreases substantially if the individual experienced either UI or welfare training in the past.

4.3.4 Exits from OLF

The results presented in the following panel relate to the OLF state. Recall that this state includes individuals that are truly out of the labour force but may also include full-time students and non-entitled unemployed workers. Caution must thus be exercised in interpreting these results.
Surprisingly many parameter estimates turn out to be statistically significant. Of particular interest, transitions from OLF to employment appear to be quite sensitive to the economic environment. Transitions to employment are thus less when the minimum wage rate or the welfare benefits increase. Similarly, the transitions into welfare and welfare training are relatively sensitive to policy variables. As in previous panels, the transitions into welfare training are more likely for those who have previously experienced such training.
For the sake of brevity, the estimation results for training programs are not presented but are available upon request. The econometric model generally does a poorer job at predicting transitions from the training programs compared to those for other states of the labour market, although a number of parameter estimates are statistically significant.

4.3.5 Unobserved heterogeneity

Table 5 reports the value of the likelihood function for a number of different specifications as well as the parameter estimates related to the unobserved heterogeneity of each. As

	No Het	Non-Para	Log-Normal	Weibull 2 Factors	Weibull 2 Factors	Weibull 3 Factors
Probability		$0.614^{\dagger}$				
ω_1		$-1.866^{\dagger}$				
ω_2		$-2.364^{\dagger}$				
b_2		-0.116	-0.221	-0.365	-0.184	$-2.980^{\dagger}$
b_3		$3.757^{\dagger}$	$7.781^{\dagger}$	$8.304^{\dagger}$	$8.209^{\dagger}$	$8.173^{\dagger}$
b_4		$2.337^{\dagger}$	$5.455^{\dagger}$	$6.201^{\dagger}$	$6.037^{\dagger}$	$8.879^{\dagger}$
b_5		1.323	0.447	0.244	-1.091	-1.691
b_6		$2.585^{\dagger}$	$5.493^{\dagger}$	$6.432^{\dagger}$	$6.168^{\dagger}$	$7.722^{\dagger}$
b_7		$-1.180^{\dagger}$	$-2.501^{\dagger}$	$-2.938^{\dagger}$	$-2.876^{\dagger}$	$-4.902^{\dagger}$
b'_1						$2.768^{\dagger}$
b'_2						$3.093^{\dagger}$
b'_3						$-7.131^{\dagger}$
b'_4						0.333
b'_5						$-8.563^{\dagger}$
b'_6						-0.437
b'_7						$0.738^{\dagger}$
μ			$-1.629^{\dagger}$			
σ			$-0.566^{\dagger}$			
λ				$9.493^{\dagger}$	$9.057^{\dagger}$	$14.685^{\dagger}$
γ				$0.163^{\dagger}$	$0.147^{\dagger}$	$0.216^{\dagger}$
Log-likelihood	-150668.6	-149774.2	-149847.8	-149818.9	-149474.8	149422.6

Table 5. Heterogeneity Parameters

†*Statistically significant at 5%*
‡*Statistically significant at 10%*

mentioned earlier, the slope parameters of these specifications are sufficiently similar to omit them from the tables.[16]

The first specification of the table does not control for unobserved heterogeneity and is thus a special case of all the other specifications. A simple likelihood-ratio test strongly rejects the first specification in favour of any specification that includes unobserved heterogeneity. The second specification is a standard non-parametric two-factor loading model and was presented in equation (4). Most parameter estimates are statistically significant, except for b_2 and b_5 which concern transitions into welfare training programs and UI training programs, respectively. Accordingly, these estimates suggest there is little, if any, selectivity into these two training programs.

The third column of the table reports the parameter estimates of a parametric two-factor loading model. As was mentioned earlier, the weibull distribution function was preferred over all other distribution functions that were investigated. Notice that as in the non-parametric specification, only b_2 and b_5 are not statistically significant. The last two lines of the table report the parameter estimates of the weibull distribution, λ and γ.[17] Finally, the last column of the table presents the parameter estimates of the three-factor

[16] Bonnal et al. (1997) also found the slope parameters to be relatively insensitive to the distributional assumptions of the unobserved heterogeneity variables. In their work, they compare a two-factor loading model with a finite number of points of support with a single-factor loading model that draws heterogeneity terms from an i.i.d. $N(0,1)$ distribution. The insensitivity of the slope parameters to the distributional assumption is consistent with the results of Heckman & Singer (1984) using single durations data.

[17] The weibull distribution function of a random variable x is given by $F(x) = 1 - \exp\left[-\lambda x^{\gamma}\right]$.

	Welfare	Welf. Tr.	JRP	UI	UI Tr.	Employ.	OLF
	TWO-FACTOR LOADING MODEL – NON-PARAMETRIC						
Welfare	1.000	-0.157	0.982	0.954	0.875	0.962	-0.850
		(0.195)	(0.010)	(0.010)	(0.236)	(0.007)	(0.023)
Wel. Tr.		1.000	0.035	0.145	0.340	0.118	0.653
			(0.200)	(0.197)	(0.495)	(0.196)	(0.150)
JRP			1.000	0.994	0.952	0.997	-0.734
				(0.006)	(0.151)	(0.004)	(0.051)
UI				1.000	0.980	1.000	-0.654
					(0.098)	(0.001)	(0.052)
UI Tr.					1.000	0.974	-0.489
						(0.111)	(0.430)
Emplo.						1.000	-0.675
							(0.048)
	TWO-FACTOR LOADING MODEL – LOG-NORMAL DISTRIBUTION						
Welfare	1.000	-0.216	0.992	0.984	0.408	0.984	-0.929
		(0.263)	(0.004)	(0.004)	(1.680)	(0.004)	(0.015)
Wel. Tr.		1.000	-0.089	-0.036	0.803	-0.037	0.563
			(0.271)	(0.272)	(1.108)	(0.272)	(0.221)
JRP			1.000	0.999	0.521	0.999	-0.874
				(0.002)	(1.571)	(0.002)	(0.029)
U.I.				1.000	0.566	1.000	-0.846
					(1.516)	(0.000)	(0.032)
UI Tr.					1.000	0.565	-0.040
						(1.518)	(1.841)
Emplo.						1.000	-0.847
							(0.031)

Table 6. Correlations Between Heterogeneity Variables
(Standard Errors in Parentheses)

loading model (see equation(6)), whose slope parameters were presented in Table 4. A simple log-likelihood ratio test rejects the two-factor loading model in favour of the three-factor loading model. Contrary to the two previous specifications, b_2 is now highly statistically significant. Furthermore, nearly all the b_j' parameters are statistically significant. This suggests that the richer specification may be better suited to uncover selection into the different states. In order to investigate this issue, Table 6 reports the correlation coefficients between the heterogeneity variables that are implicit in each specification along with their standard errors. The first two panels focus on the non-parametric and the weibull two-factor loading models. Recall that these correlation coefficients indicate the extent to which one is as likely to enter state j as state k upon leaving any given state. While a number of coefficients are similar across both panels, there are significant differences. To start with, the first line of each panel shows that high transition rates into welfare are associated with lower transition rates into welfare training and higher rates into unemployment. On the other hand, both panels disagree significantly with respect to the correlations between welfare training and the other states, as well as between JRP and other states. The non-parametric model implies that welfare training and UI training are positively correlated whereas the opposite holds true in the parametric model. Similarly, the top panel indicates that JRP is positively correlated to all other states on the labour market, contrary to the parametric model which shows no such relations.

The last panel of Table 6 focuses on the correlation coefficients implicit in the three-factor loading model. Each section of the panel is related to the correlation coefficients in equations

	Welfare	Welf. Tr.	JRP	UI	UI Tr.	Employ.	OLF
	TWO-FACTOR LOADING MODEL						
	WEIBULL DISTRIBUTION - NO DUMMY INDICATORS						
Welfare	1.000	-0.343	0.993	0.987	0.237	0.988	-0.947
		(0.266)	(0.004)	(0.004)	(2.413)	(0.003)	(0.012)
Wel. Tr.		1.000	-0.228	-0.189	0.832	-0.195	0.627
			(0.278)	(0.281)	(1.390)	(0.280)	(0.218)
JRP			1.000	0.999	0.351	0.999	-0.901
				(0.001)	(2.325)	(0.001)	(0.026)
U.I.				1.000	0.388	1.000	-0.883
					(2.288)		(0.027)
UI Tr.					1.000	0.383	0.089
						(2.294)	(2.475)
Emplo.						1.000	-0.886
							(0.026)
	TWO-FACTOR LOADING MODEL						
	WEIBULL DISTRIBUTION - WITH DUMMY INDICATORS						
Welfare	1.000	-0.181	0.993	0.987	-0.737	0.987	-0.945
		(0.337)	(0.004)	(0.004)	(0.943)	(0.003)	(0.013)
Wel. Tr.		1.000	-0.061	-0.018	0.798	-0.021	0.494
			(0.341)	(0.344)	(0.872)	(0.344)	(0.296)
JRP			1.000	0.999	-0.650	0.999	-0.898
				(0.002)	(1.062)	(0.001)	(0.027)
U.I.				1.000	-0.617	1.000	-0.878
					(1.098)	(0.000)	(0.028)
UI Tr.					1.000	-0.619	0.918
						(1.096)	(0.552)
Emplo.						1.000	-0.880
							(0.027)

Table 6. (Continued)
Correlations Between Heterogeneity Variables
(Standard Errors in Parentheses)

(7)–(9), respectively. Hence, the first section has the same interpretation as the correlations of the previous panels. The correlation coefficients reported in this section differ considerably from the previous ones. According to the estimates, it now appears that there is considerable selectivity into welfare training as well as in JRP. Indeed, those who are more likely to participate in the former are also more likely to train under JRP and to find employment. On the other hand, higher transition rates into JRP or welfare training is now associated with lower transition rates into UI and UI training. This is in stark contrast with the previous results. Other correlation coefficients are relatively similar to the previous ones.

The second section of the panel reports the correlation coefficients with respect to the origin states. Large heterogeneity values in the origin state translate into short spell durations. Consequently, the correlations reflect the frequency with which individuals transit across the various states. The estimates show that individuals who are more likely to have long welfare spells are also likely to have short employment spells. The same holds with respect to welfare training and employment, as well as JRP and employment. Those who are more likely to have short unemployment spells are more likely to have long JRP, welfare training or UI training spells.

	Welfare	Welf. Tr.	JRP	UI	UI Tr.	Employ.	OLF
	CORRELATION BETWEEN DESTINATION STATES						
Welfare	1.000	-0.948	0.993	0.994	-0.861	0.992	-0.980
		(0.026)	(0.006)	(0.002)	(0.568)	(0.002)	(0.007)
Wel. Tr.		1.000	-0.902	-0.906	0.978	-0.899	0.992
			(0.042)	(0.038)	(0.232)	(0.040)	(0.007)
JRP			1.000	0.998	-0.792	0.998	-0.948
				(0.001)	(0.682)	(0.000)	(0.020)
UI				1.000	-0.798	0.999	-0.951
					(0.672)	(0.001)	(0.014)
UI Tr.					1.000	-0.788	0.945
						(0.687)	(0.363)
Emplo.						1.000	-0.946
							(0.015)
	CORRELATION BETWEEN ORIGIN STATES						
Welfare	1.000	0.951	-0.990	0.316	-0.993	-0.401	0.594
		(0.027)	(0.006)	(0.756)	(0.006)	(0.369)	(0.197)
Wel. Tr.		1.000	-0.900	0.592	-0.909	-0.099	0.812
			(0.046)	(0.622)	(0.045)	(0.374)	(0.123)
JRP			1.000	-0.181	1.000	0.524	-0.476
				(0.784)	(0.002)	(0.346)	(0.223)
U.I.				1.000	-0.204	0.743	0.951
					(0.782)	(0.467)	(0.225)
UI Tr.					1.000	0.504	-0.496
						(0.350)	(0.221)
Emplo.						1.000	0.500
							(0.310)
	CORRELATION BETWEEN ORIGIN-DESTINATION STATES						
Welfare	1.000	0.951	-0.990	0.316	-0.993	-0.401	0.594
		(0.027)	(0.006)	(0.756)	(0.006)	(0.369)	(0.197)
Wel. Tr.	-0.948	-0.902	0.939	-0.299	0.942	0.380	-0.563
	(0.026)	(0.044)	(0.028)	(0.720)	(0.028)	(0.345)	(0.197)
JRP	0.993	0.944	-0.983	0.313	-0.986	-0.398	0.589
	(0.006)	(0.028)	(0.009)	(0.751)	(0.009)	(0.367)	(0.196)
UI	0.994	0.946	-0.984	0.314	-0.987	-0.398	0.590
	(0.002)	(0.028)	(0.007)	(0.751)	(0.007)	(0.367)	(0.196)
UI Tr.	-0.861	-0.819	0.852	-0.272	0.855	0.345	-0.511
	(0.568)	(0.544)	(0.563)	(0.725)	(0.565)	(0.367)	(0.395)
Emplo.	0.992	0.944	-0.982	0.313	-0.985	-0.397	0.589
	(0.002)	(0.028)	(0.007)	(0.750)	(0.007)	(0.366)	(0.196)
OLF	-0.980	-0.932	0.970	-0.309	0.973	0.392	-0.582
	(0.007)	(0.031)	(0.010)	(0.742)	(0.010)	(0.360)	(0.196)

Table 6. (Continued) Correlations Between Heterogeneity Variables
Three-Factor Loading Model
(Standard Errors in Parentheses)

The last section of the panel reports the implicit correlations between the origin and the destination states. Note that the correlation matrix need not be symmetric nor does the diagonal need be equal to unity. On the other hand, the restrictions that were imposed to achieve identification of the loading parameters imply that the first row of the matrix is equal to the first row of the matrix of the middle section.

For the sake of brevity we will focus our attention on the most interesting correlations. The estimates suggest that those who are likely to have short welfare training spells are also less likely to transit through welfare or JRP and more likely to enter employment (row 2). Similarly, row 3 indicates that individuals who are likely to have short JRP spells are less likely to return to either welfare or welfare training in the future, and much more likely to enter employment. Finally, those who have short UI training spells (row 5) have higher transitions rates into welfare and welfare training, and lower transitions rates into employment.

These correlations suggest there is considerable selectivity into the training programs. Furthermore, they show that those who are selected into welfare and JRP training programs appear to be different from those who participate in UI training programs. As a matter of fact, all the correlation coefficients of the last section of the panel pertaining to UI training have the opposite sign to those of welfare and JRP training. Consider, for example, those who have unexpectedly long UI training spells and those who have unexpectedly short welfare training or JRP spells. According to the last section of the panel, all these individuals are more likely to move into employment upon exiting their respective spells than average. Yet, the middle section indicates that only those on welfare training or JRP are likely to have long employment spells. Those who were on UI training are more likely to have short employment spells.

That those who are likely to have short JRP or welfare training spells are more likely to experiment long employment spells may be somewhat surprising. In fact, when studying the impact of the Youth Training Scheme in the UK, Mealli et al. (1996) and Mealli & Pudney (2003) conjectured that early program termination may result from more intensive search stemming from better than average motivation. Hence, early termination may be associated with a higher probability of transition into employment and longer employment spells. Conversely, if failure to complete the full term is a consequence of low ability and motivation, it may be associated with poorer employment outcomes. Although we have no information regarding program completion, our results are consistent with the first possibility, whereas those of Mealli et al. (1996) were consistent with the second possibility.

5. Conclusion

The analysis has focused on an examination of the impact of government-sponsored training programs aimed at disadvantaged male youths on their labour market transitions. We have elected to concentrate our attention on this group since they have fared relatively poorly on the labour market over the past decade in Canada by all accounts. The richness of the data at our disposal has allowed us to recreate very detailed individual histories over a relatively long period. As many as seven distinct states on the labour market could be identified in the data.

This study has applied a continuous time duration model to estimate the density of duration times in these seven states, controlling for the endogeneity of an individual's training status. Most previous studies have used survey or administrative data that were less amenable to the kind of analysis performed in this chapter. Depending on the nature of the data, complex adjustments to the model were often required to account for potential problems related to stock sampling and initial conditions. Fortunately, we were able to avoid these difficulties by recreating each individual's history as early as age 16, the legal school-leaving age in Canada. Consequently, the initial state can be safely considered exogenous, and the subsequent duration times void of any form of bias.

There is no consensus in the literature concerning the appropriate treatment of unobserved heterogeneity in multi-states multi-episodes duration models. When few states are considered, two-factor loading models with a finite set of points of support have become relatively standard. When the analysis focuses on more states, factor loading models require a large number of parameters to be flexible or become relatively restrictive if a parsimonious specification is used. In this chapter we have chosen to investigate the sensitivity of the parameter estimates by comparing a typical non-parametric specification and a series of parametric two-factor loading models. These models implicitly assume that the intensity of transitions are related to the state of destination. We have also estimated a parametric three-factor loading model. The novelty of this specification lies in the fact that the intensities of transitions are related to both to the state of destination and the state of origin.

The estimation of the model yields a number of interesting results. As found in previous studies, unobserved heterogeneity appears to play an important role in determining who selects or gets selected in training programs. On the other hand, the slope and baseline hazard parameter estimates are not very sensitive to the choice of a particular distribution function for the unobserved heterogeneity variables. The two-factor loading models, either parametric or non-parametric, yield essentially the same results as the three-factor loading model. These show that the duration times in any of the seven states considered are sensitive to variations in program parameters such as welfare benefits, policy variables such as the minimum wage rate, and in the economic environment as proxied by the unemployment rate. Nearly all the parameter estimates have the expected sign when statistically significant.

The results pertaining to the impact of the welfare training programs and JRP are similar to those found earlier by Gritz (1993), Bonnal et al. (1997) and Fortin et al. (1999a). In essence, young, poorly educated males who participate in these programs do not fair as well on the labour market compared to non-participants, even after controlling for unobserved heterogeneity. On the other hand, participation in training programs while on unemployment insurance provides them some benefits in the form of increased transitions into employment.

6. References

Beaudry, P. & Green, D. A. (2000). Cohort patterns in canadian earnings: assessing the role of skill premia in inequality trends, *Canadian Journal of Economics* 33: 907–936.

Blasco, S., Crépon, B. & Kamionka, T. (2009). *Evaluation of the Impact of Training on Individual Labor Market Transitions*, Mimeo, Crest, Paris.

Bonnal, L., Fougère, D. & Sérandon, A. (1997). Evaluating the impact of french employment policies on individual labour market histories, *The Review of Economics Studies* 64(4): 683–718.

Brouillette, D. & Lacroix, G. (2010). Heterogeneous treatment and self-selection in a wage subsidy experiment, *Journal of Public Economics* 94(7-8): 479 – 492.

Brouillette, D. & Lacroix, G. (2011). Assessing the impact of a wage subsidy for single parents on social assistance in canada, *Canadian Journal of Economics*, Forthcoming.

Burtless, G. (1995). The case for randomized field trials in economic and policy research, *Journal of Economic Perspective* 9(2): 63–84.

Card, D. & Hyslop, D. (2005). Estimating the effects of a time-limited earnings subsidy for welfare leavers, *Econometrica* 73.

Card, D. & Hyslop, D. R. (2009). The dynamic effects of an earnings subsidy for long-term welfare recipients: Evidence from the self sufficiency project applicant experiment, *Journal of Econometrics* 153(1): 1 – 20.

Crépon, B., Gurgand, M., Kamionka, T. & Lequien, L. (2011). Is counseling welfare recipients cost-effective ? Lessons from a random experiment, Mimeo, CREST, Paris.

Doiron, D. & Gorgens, T. (2008). State dependence in youth labor market experiences, and the evaluation of policy interventions, *Journal of Econometrics* 145: 81–97.

Duclos, J.-Y., Fortin, B., Lacroix, G. & Roberge, H. (1999). The dynamics of welfare participation in Québec, *in* P. L. & R. Chaykowsky (eds), *Women and Work*, The John Deutch Institute.

Edon, C. & Kamionka, T. (2007). Modélisation dynamique de la participation au marché du travail des femmes en couple, *Annales d'économie et de statistique* 86: 77–108.

Fortin, B., Fougère, D. & Lacroix, G. (1999a). Hausse des barèmes et sorties de l'aide sociale: Les résultats d'une expérience naturelle au Canada, *Revue Économique* pp. 451–463.

Fortin, B., Fougère, D. & Lacroix, G. (1999b). The impact of government-sponsored training programs on labour market transitions, Prepared for Human Resources Development Canada.

Fortin, B., Lacroix, G. & Drolet, S. (2004). Welfare benefits and the duration of welfare spells: evidence from a natural experiment in canada, *Journal of Public Economics* 88(7-8): 1495 – 1520.

Fougère, D. & Kamionka, T. (2008). Econometrics of individual labor market transitions, *in* L. Mátyás & P. Sevestre (eds), *The Econometrics of Panel Data*, Advanced Studies in Theoretical and Applied Econometrics, Springer, pp. 865–905.

Fougère, D., Kamionka, T. & Priéto, A. (2010). L'efficacité des mesures d'accompagnement sur le retour à l'emploi, *Revue Economique* 61(3): 599–612.

Gouriéroux, C. & Monfort, A. (1992). Modèles de durée et effets de génération, *Working Paper # 9125*, CREST, Paris.

Gourriéroux, C. & Monfort, A. (1991). Simulation based econometrics in models with heterogeneity, *Annales d'économie et de statistique* 20(1): 69–107.

Gritz, R. (1993). The impact of training on the frequency and the duration of employment, *Journal of Econometrics* 57: 21–51.

Ham, J. & LaLonde, R. (1996). The effect of sample selection and intitial conditions in duration models: Evidence from experimental data on training, *Econometrica* 64(1): 175–205.

Ham, J. & Rea, S. (1987). Unemployment insurance and male unemployment duration in canada, *Journal of Human Resources* pp. 325–353.

Heckman, J. & Flinn, C. (1983). Are unemployment and out of the labor force beheviorally distinct labor force states ?, *Journal of Labor Economics* 1(1).

Heckman, J., LaLonde, R. & Smith, J. (1999). The economics and econometrics of active labor market programs, *in* O. Ashenfelter & E. D. Card (eds), *Handbook of Labor Economics*, North-Holland, chapter.

Heckman, J. & Singer, B. (1984). A method for minimizing the distributional assumptions in econometric models for duration data, *Econometrica* pp. 271–320.

Heckman, J. & Smith, J. (1995). Assessing the case for social experiments, *Journal of Economic Perspective* 9(2): 85–110.

Jones, S. & Riddell, C. (1999). The measurement of unemployment: An empirical approach, *Econometrica* 67(1): 147–61.

Kamionka, T. (1998). Simulated maximum likelihood estimation in transition models, *Econometrics Journal* 1: C129–C153.

Kamionka, T. & Lacroix, G. (2008). Assessing the external validity of an experimental wage subsidy, *Annales d'Économie et de Statistique* 357–384.

Keane, M. P. (2010). A structural perspective on the experimentalist school, *Journal of Economic Perspectives* 24(2): 47–58.

Laroque, G. & Salanié, B. (1993). Simulation-based estimation of models with lagged latent variables, *Journal of Applied Econometrics* 8: S119–S133.

Leamer, E. E. (2010). Tantalus on the road to asymptopia, *Journal of Economic Perspectives* 24(2): 31–46.

Mealli, F. & Pudney, S. (2003). Applying heterogenous transition models in labour economics: The role of youth training in labour market transitions, *in* R. Chambers & C. Skinner (eds), *Analysis of Survey Data*, John Wiley and Sons, chapter 16, pp. 245–274.

Mealli, F., Pudney, S. & Thomas, J. (1996). Training duration and post-training outcomes: A duration-limited competing risks model, *Economic Journal* 106(435): 422–433.

Van den Berg, G. (1997). Association measures for durations in bivariate hazard rate models, *Journal of Econometrics* 79(2): 221–245.

Van den Berg, G., Lindeboom, M. & Ridder, G. (1994). Attrition in longitudinal panel data, and the empirical analysis of dynamic labour market behaviour, *Journal of Applied Econometrics* 9: 421–435.

5

Returns to Education and Experience Within the EU: An Instrumental Variable Approach for Panel Data

Inmaculada García-Mainar and Víctor M. Montuenga-Gómez
University of Zaragoza
Spain

1. Introduction

Estimating the returns to education and experience has been a topic for labour economists for decades, with a significant volume of research being devoted to appraising the causal effect of schooling on earnings. One central interest when estimating these returns has been to study whether differences exist across several demographic sectors; essentially, distinguishing between males and females, whites and non-whites, or natives and immigrants, to assess the possibility of wage discrimination, and to compute the extent of the wage gap between the groups (Harmon et al., 2003).

A rapidly growing literature examines differences in the return to education, distinguishing between the self-employed and wage earners (Evans & Leighton, 1989; Hamilton, 2000; Lazear & Moore, 1984; Rees & Shah, 1986). Fundamentally, these studies have set out not only to investigate earning differentials between the two employment groups *per se*, but also to test competing views about the relationship between earnings and education, on the basis that these groups are subject to different economic incentives. In this context, the self-employed can be used as a control group to distinguish between human capital and sorting models of wage determination, assuming that signaling or screening functions are much less relevant for the self-employed (Riley, 1979; Wolpin, 1977). Returns to experience for the self-employed have also been estimated against those for wage earners, in order to test different theories of the labor market, such as those of agency and risk hypotheses, against the learning and matching models, and against the compensating differentials premises, for example. Thus, so long as the self-employed have fewer incentives to shirk on the job, or to quit it, they should exhibit flatter earnings-experience profiles, since wage earners obtain higher earnings than the self-employed as they grow older (Salop and Salop, 1976).

In this chapter, we set out to estimate the returns to education and to experience for both the self-employed and wage earners, with our aim being to address some of the issues raised above. In doing so, we provide evidence of such returns for three EU countries, namely Germany, Italy and the UK, using panel data information. Examining cross-country data is helpful in identifying common features that are not considered in a single-country analysis. Moreover, these countries cover a wide range of variation across Europe. Germany represents those countries with self-employment rates well below the EU average; Italy is an example of those Southern and peripheral countries with self-employment rates over 20%, and the UK stands for those countries exhibiting the average. Table 1 shows the 20-year evolution of the self-employment rate within the EU-15.

	1987	1995	2000	2007
Austria	-	10.8	10.5	14.4
Belgium	15.3	15.4	13.6	12.8
Denmark	9.2	8.4	8.0	8.9
Finland	-	14.3	12.6	12.6
France	12.7	11.6	10.0	9.0
Germany	9.1	9.4	9.7	12.0
Greece	35.4	33.8	31.3	35.9
Ireland	21.8	20.8	16.5	16.8
Italy	24.4	24.5	23.6	26.4
Luxembourg	9.2	10.0	8.7	6.1
Netherlands	10.1	11.5	10.0	12.4
Portugal	27.2	25.8	20.2	24.2
Spain	23.5	21.8	18.0	17.7
Sweden	-	11.3	9.8	10.6
United Kingdom	12.5	13.0	10.9	13.8
EU15	15.9	15.0	13.6	15.6

Table 1. Self-employment rates (Eurostat Labour Force Survey). Note: Percentage of self-employed persons over total employed.

Using a homogeneous database, we investigate whether differences exist in the profitability of schooling and experience, both between the two employment statuses, and across the three sample countries. The database used in this work has been obtained from the European Community Household Panel (ECHP), from 1994 to 2000, which provides abundant information about the personal and labour characteristics of individuals, and has the advantage that this information is homogeneous across the sample countries, given that the questionnaire is the same and the collection process is coordinated by the Statistical Office of the European Community (EUROSTAT). Additionally, the application of panel data techniques offers some clear advantages over the traditional cross-sectional approaches. First, individual unobserved heterogeneity is controlled for. Second, biases arising from aggregation, selectivity, measurement error, and endogeneity can be dealt with in an appropriate form. Third, dynamic behavior, such as the movements into and out of self-employment, may be explicitly accounted for.

The two usual estimators used in panel data, that is to say fixed and random effects, are, however, inadequate in this setting if the objective is to obtain consistent and efficient measures of the profitability of education and experience. Thus, the presence of time-invariant and possibly endogenous regressors (e.g. education), would make it impossible to estimate their associated parameters when a time or mean-differencing approach, i.e. the fixed effects, is applied. Additionally, the probable correlation between these time-invariant regressors and the unobserved effects causes the random effects estimator to be inconsistent. Altogether, this points to the advisability of using a hybrid technique that lies between both extremes. Moreover, the potential existence of measurement errors and/or endogeneity requires instrumental variables (IV) to obtain consistent estimates of the coefficients. As a consequence, the Hausman & Taylor (1981) estimator is the most adequate, since it has been shown to be an Efficient Generalised Instrumental Variable (EGIV). This procedure allows simultaneous control for the correlation between regressors and unobserved individual effects (as fixed effects) and to identify the estimates for the time-invariant covariates, such as education, as a random effects estimator. Furthermore, it eliminates the uncertainty associated with the choice of instruments, since exogenous included variables, and their means over time, are used as efficient instruments.

Our results show that returns to education are greater for workers in paid work, with non-linearities in the relationship between wages and educational levels (the so-called sheepskin effect). Both findings point to the relevance of signalling in the earnings of workers. Earnings experience profiles are, however, not very different across groups, especially when experience is not very great, indicating absence of delays in remuneration for workers.

The rest of the chapter is structured as follows. In the next section, we consider the theoretical aspects of the returns to education and experience. Section 3 is devoted to the empirical model and to a discussion of the estimation procedure, the EGIV technique proposed in Hausman and Taylor (1981). Section 4 describes the data in the sample countries. Section 5 offers the estimates of the rates of return and examines the differences across countries to cast some light on labour-status differences. Finally, Section 6 provides a summary of the main results.

2. Theoretical aspects of returns to schooling and experience in relation to self-employment

A new-born child enjoys an initial endowment of human capital (a conglomerate of intelligence, ability, motivation, characteristics of the social and economic environment, etc.) that can be improved upon by knowledge accumulation, both during the schooling period and through on-the-job experience. According to the human capital theory (Becker, 1962, 1964), there exists a positive relationship between investment in human capital and earnings, in such a way that a greater accumulation of human capital is rewarded in the labor market with higher earnings.

The individual chooses to stay in school until the expected marginal benefit equals the expected marginal costs of one additional year of schooling, and differences in ability among individuals cause schooling choices to also differ. Empirically, a linear relationship is usually assumed between the log of the earnings and the set of regressors. This implies that ability influences only the intercept of log-earnings. Following this reasoning, we apply the widely-used wage equation (Mincer, 1974) that can be expressed as:

$$\ln w_t = \alpha\, f(A_t) + \beta\, g(Edu_t) + \gamma\, h(Exp_t) + \eta' Char_t + \varepsilon_t \qquad (1)$$

where *w* denotes earnings, *A* the initial human capital, or ability, *Edu* is the education variable, *Exp* is the experience and *Char* a set of personal and labor characteristics (such as gender, age, occupation, type of contract, etc.) which can be time-constant or time-varying. Since ability is usually unobservable to the researcher, this must be included in the error term. However, this ability may be correlated with schooling, in such a way that standard least squares yield biased estimates (Griliches, 1977). This issue will be discussed further in Section 3.2.

Although specification (1) has been derived on the grounds of human capital theory, competing perspectives may generate similar conclusions. In particular, the sorting or signaling model also predicts that higher earnings are positively related to higher educational attainments. However, in this case, greater human capital does not lead to higher productivity (and thus, higher earnings), but greater human capital is acquired in order to signal higher productivity (Spence, 1973; Stiglitz, 1975). In other words, firms do not reward productivity in a direct way because this is not observed *a priori*; rather, they infer productivity from education, and students choose an education level to signal their productivity to potential employers. Similarly, firms offer higher wages for the highly educated, since education acts as a screening device, so long as education is positively correlated with the unobserved productivity.

As a consequence, estimating equation (1) does not help to discriminate between human capital and the sorting models; while it may be viewed as a good approach to assessing the effect of schooling on earnings, it is not completely satisfactory in elucidating which view prevails in the process of wage determination (Weiss, 1995). However, considering the self-employed as a control group may serve as a device to investigate the question, since signaling and screening purposes seem to be unimportant for this group of workers (Riley, 1979; Wolpin, 1977). The null hypothesis adopted by these authors is that returns to education will be higher in those occupations that exhibit signaling, on the basis that it is difficult to reconcile the idea that education for the self-employed could act as a sorting mechanism. As a consequence, returns to schooling for those in paid employment should be higher, since those individuals benefit from the dual effect of education: the productive and the informative functions. By contrast, the self-employed are only remunerated for the productive nature of education and, thus, returns are lower.

However, although the theoretical implications seem quite clear-cut, the empirical evidence is not conclusive. Focusing on the US, some authors report that self-employed earnings are less responsive to human capital variables than wage-employed earnings (Hamilton, 2000), thereby favouring the sorting hypothesis., whereas others (Evans and Jovanovic, 1989; Evans and Leighton, 1989; Kawaguchi, 2003) find that self-employed earnings equations have larger schooling coefficients than those corresponding to the wage-employed, rejecting the sorting hypothesis.

Distinguishing between self-employed and wage-earner returns may also be helpful in providing insights into the features of theoretical labour market models. Thus, studying the experience profile in earnings may serve to ascertain whether agency issues, learning and matching models, or compensating differentials theory, for example, better fit the labour market. A number of studies predict that earnings-experience profiles are flatter for the self-employed. Under the agency or risk theories (Lazear, 1981; Lazear & Moore, 1984), employers should pay less than the marginal productivity to workers when they are young, and more when they grow older, to avoid shirking on the job, contrary to the case of the self-employed, given that these individuals have no incentive to shirk. Similarly, asymmetric information models (Salop & Salop, 1976) argue that, because employers are interested in minimizing the quits of more productive workers, they offer tilted-up wage profiles as a screening device, in such a way that only workers with low probabilities of quitting apply for jobs. By contrast, since the self-employed are not willing to quit, they have flatter earnings profiles than those of wage earners. In the same vein, learning models claim that, due to sector-specific abilities that are unknown for the individual, workers may not match themselves to the appropriate sector. Those who realize they have a poor match quit their jobs, and only those with relatively good matches stay. This situation causes experience profiles to increase over time (Jovanovic, 1979, 1982). Furthermore, since the self-employed habitually invest strongly at the start-up of their businesses, they are not able to move out of

their poor match, and therefore their experience profiles are flatter (Dunn & Holt-Eakin, 2000). All of these studies suggest steeper experience profiles for wage earners, especially at the very end of the years of experience distribution, to ensure long seniority in the firm.
Contrary results, however, are found in the investment model, for example, which validates the claim that the self-employed obtain steeper earnings profiles because physical and human capital investments are not shared with an employer (Hashimoto, 1981). Similarly, steeper earning profiles of the self-employed can be observed in the cases where average returns to experience are distorted by the existence of a few, but very successful, entrepreneurs (the so-called "superstars"), whereas the bulk of the self-employed remain with low returns or leave for paid employment (Rosen, 1981).
In summary, undisputed conclusions about the magnitude of the returns to education and experience for the self-employed and for salaried employees have not been achieved. The majority of prior analyses have focused on investigating only one country, without offering any kind of comparative study. Furthermore, only a limited number of articles have used data for a period of more than one year. Even when they have done so, they have estimated returns by pooling the data, an approach which does not allow for control for the unobserved characteristics of the individuals, nor for movements into or out of self-employment. Additionally, only the recent availability of panel data and the development of new statistical packages have permitted the application of EGIV techniques in order to gain efficiency in estimations. The aim of this chapter is precisely to address some of these gaps in the literature by computing returns to education and experience for a set of EU countries, using information provided in panel data form, which are statistically efficient.

3. The empirical model and estimation procedure

This section focuses on the empirical specification of the earnings equation and the methodology used for its estimation. The first sub-section is devoted to determining the most appropriate empirical model for our study, while the second describes the logic supporting the use of the Hausman-Taylor procedure in the estimation.

3.1 Empirical specification

As discussed in Section 2, estimates of the returns to education and experience for the self-employed and wage earners are usually obtained from Mincer-type wage regressions. Dating from the mid 20th century, a body of empirical work has investigated these returns across countries on the basis of such a specification (Psacharapoulos, 1973, 1981, 1985, 1994; Trostel et al., 2002). Cross-sectional information has normally been used, with the IV approach, progressively substituting for the traditional OLS estimation to account for endogeneity and ability biases, as well as measurement errors. This has resulted in estimates of the rates of return well above those obtained from OLS (Card, 1999, 2001).
Our estimated model is an extended version of the Mincerian-baseline equation (1), in which earnings rewarding more education can be seen as the combined effect of human capital accumulation and the effect of being identified as a graduate rather than as a dropout. It takes the following form:

$$\ln w_{it} = \beta Edu_i + \mu_1 Exp_{it} + \mu_2 Exp^2_{it}/100 + X'_{it}\,\delta + Z'_i\,\gamma + u_{it}, \qquad (2)$$

where *i* and *t* stand for the *N* individuals and the *T* time periods, respectively. As indicated before, *w* denotes earnings; *Edu* is the education variable (that is considered time-invariant);

Exp is the experience; *X* is a set of time-varying regressors, and *Z* is a set of time-invariant regressors. The β coefficient expresses the rate of return to education; μ_1 and μ_2 represent the earnings-experience profile, and δ and γ are the set of parameters accompanying the remaining regressors.

Rather than using the education measure normally employed in the literature, years of schooling, we consider the educational attainment of each worker, providing two clear advantages. First, it does not impose the annual marginal effect of schooling as being the same in each year of education, and second, the level of education is a more appropriate measure, since multiple education streams characterize European countries, and salary profiles used to be largely linked to the education category attained. In other words, they capture the possibility that credentials matter more than years of schooling *per se* in the wage determination. This hypothesis is commonly known as the "sheepskin effect" and attempts to explain the discontinuous changes in earnings associated with completion of elementary school, high school or college (Belman & Heywood, 1991; Hungeford & Solon, 1987; Jaeger & Page, 1996).

Educational attainment, which is considered time-invariant in our sample, represents the last completed level of schooling, classified as primary, secondary, and high. Primary includes elementary and below elementary school, secondary includes vocational and middle school, and tertiary or high includes university studies (in either short or long cycles). Consequently, the fragment "$\beta\ Edu_i$" in equation (2) would be represented by "$\beta_1\ EduS_i + \beta_2\ EduH_i$". The category of reference is $EduP_i$, omitted in the estimation.

$$\ln w_{it} = \beta_1 \text{EduS}_i + \beta_2 \text{EduH}_i + \mu_1 \text{Exp}_{it} + \mu_2 \text{Exp}^2_{it}/100 + X'_{it}\,\delta + Z'_i\,\gamma + u_{it}, \qquad (3)$$

The dependent variable is the natural log of net earnings, where these are defined as gross earnings less tax, expressed in per hour real terms. The earnings-experience profiles are analyzed by considering the number of years that an individual has been working, and its squared value divided by 100 to take care of the decreasing returns. Specifically, experience is measured as the difference between the current age and the age of initiation at work, thereby expressing potential experience. The remaining independent variables, represented in equation (3) by *X* and *Z*, contain dummies for gender, marital status, training, occupation, sector, seniority, and a set of time fixed effects, as described in Section 4.

3.2 Estimating the earnings equation: the Hausman-Taylor procedure

The general model in (3) assumes that the error term u_{it} consists of the sum of two components, i.e. $u_{it} = a_i + v_{it}$, where a_i represents the random individual-specific effect that characterizes each worker and is constant through time, and v_{it} is a random disturbance varying over time and individuals. This latter stochastic term is assumed to be uncorrelated with all included variables. Similarly, it is also assumed that the random disturbance is a sequence of i.i.d. random variables with mean zero and variance σ^2_v; that v_{it} and α_i are mutually independent, and that α_i is i.i.d. over the panels with mean zero and variance σ^2_α. Thus, the variance-covariance matrix of the system has the random effects structure that can be represented as $E(UU') = \sigma^2_\alpha (i_T i_T' \otimes I_N) + \sigma^2_v (I_T \otimes I_N)$, where i_T is a Tx1 vector containing 1s, I_N (I_T) is the identity matrix of rank N (T), and U is an NTx1 vector of disturbances. Thus, random-effects or Generalised Leasts Squares (GLS) produce consistent estimators.

However, the presence of measurement errors and unobserved variables, such as ability, motivation, etc., that may be correlated with schooling, bias GLS estimates. Specifically, it has been shown that measurement errors bias downwards the GLS estimates (Angrist and Krueger, 1999) although recent evidence (Card, 2001) only attributes a 10% gap, at most, to this source of bias. By contrast, since schooling and any unobserved ability may be positively correlated, omitting measures of ability results in the schooling coefficient being biased upwards (Griliches, 1977). Consequently, some effort must be made to alleviate such an ability bias as much as possible. When a direct indication of ability, such as IQ score tests, or information from twins or siblings, is not available (see Ashenfelter & Krueger, 1994, and Miller et al., 1995), the most appropriate exercise is to select an instrumental variables estimator, through which schooling is instrumented with variables that are correlated with it, but not with errors. A broad range of instruments have been proposed in the literature. Typical examples are those known as natural experiments (see Rosenzweig and Wolpin, 2000, for a summary) which include: i) school reforms and features of the school system (Harmon and Walker, 1995); ii) the proximity to College of the place of residence (Card, 1995); iii) other supply-side instruments capturing features of the education system (see Card, 2001 for a survey of the literature); and iv) the season of birth of the individual (Angrist and Krueger, 1991).

When using IV in cross-sections, a common finding is that estimates are 20% higher, or even more, than OLS estimates. This is a rather unexpected result, since OLS is already believed to provide upward-biased estimates arising from the ability bias. Some reasons have been proposed to explain such a result. Apart from the positive publication bias (Ashenfelter et al., 1999), IV estimates may be biased upwards further than OLS due to the existence of unobserved differences between the characteristics of the treatment and comparison groups implicit in the IV scheme (Bound et al., 1995). Specifically, when treatment effects are used, since returns to education are heterogeneous across individuals, the IV estimates tend to recover the returns to education of the population group most affected by the intervention, so that IV estimates are then a better approximation for the returns to education of the affected group, rather than for the whole population (Card, 1999, 2001). Similarly, IV estimates will tend to be biased towards the returns to schooling attainments that are most common in the sample data (see Belzil and Hansen, 2002).

Both the available data structure and the existence of problems associated with the choice of instruments have influenced the procedure applied in this study. On the one hand, the ECHP is in panel data form, but does not provide information on IQ tests, and the presence of twins is not especially accounted for. On the other hand, although the number of alternative instruments routinely considered in the literature is sufficiently wide, their application to our data is quite complex. This has led us to consider an alternative procedure for estimation, in which the availability of panel data is taken into account, namely the IV-type model proposed by Hausman and Taylor (1981). Our selection of this procedure is motivated by several considerations. As is well known, the availability of panel data allows us to control for individual unobserved heterogeneity (possibly correlated with other included variables), since this factor may be eliminated by mean or time-differencing, i.e. by applying a fixed effects-type estimator (Polachek & Kim, 1994). Although this within estimator is probably not fully-efficient, it produces consistent estimates. However, when operating in this way, coefficients of the time-constant variables (e.g. the level of education) cannot be estimated, since they disappear when mean or time-differences are constructed. For its part, a pure random effects estimator, the GLS, produces biased and inconsistent estimates, assuming as it does that there is no correlation between any of the regressors and

the individual effects. In our case, the GLS estimator is not valid because education and experience may be correlated with individual effects.
One way to obtain consistent estimates of the returns to education and experience would be to find instruments for these variables which are potentially correlated with the individual effects. The choice of the appropriate instruments is, however, not an easy task, since the use of instruments that are weakly correlated with endogenous variables may produce downward-biased estimates, even with large samples (see Bound et al, 1995; Chamberlain & Imbens, 2004; Staiger & Stock, 1997), generating uncertainty in the selection of instruments. Consequently, what we require is a procedure that controls for the endogeneity of education (and possibly other variables), but which is still able to recover the coefficient of time-invariant regressors. Hausman & Taylor (1981) propose a model where some of the regressors may be correlated with individual effects, as opposed to the random effects model, where no regressor can be correlated with the individual effect, and to the fixed effects model, where all the regressors may be correlated with individual effects. If, in addition, this procedure does not require instruments excluded in the regression but the instruments used are precisely those included in the wage regression, the Hausman-Taylor estimator is, potentially, the best choice.
This Hausman-Taylor estimator is an instrumental variables estimator that uses both the between and within variations of the strictly exogenous variables as instruments. More specifically, the individual means of the strictly exogenous regressors are used as instruments for the time invariant regressors correlated with individual effects. This procedure is implemented in the following steps. First, equation (3) is estimated by pooled Two Stages Least Squares (2SLS), where the set of variables mentioned above act as instruments. Second, the pooled 2SLS residuals are used to obtain estimates of σ^2_α and σ^2_v, which can then be used to construct the weights for a Feasible Generalized Least Squares estimator. Third, these weights are used to transform (by quasi-time demeaning) all the dependent, explanatory, and instrumental variables. Finally, the transformed regression is again estimated by pooled 2SLS, where the individual means, over time, of the time-varying regressors, and the exogenous time-invariant regressors, are the instruments. Under the full set of assumptions mentioned in the previous sub-section, this Hausman and Taylor estimator becomes an Efficient Generalized Instrumental Variables (EGIV) and coincides with the efficient GMM estimator.
Formally, the Hausman-Taylor model can be represented in its most general form as follows:

$$\ln w_{it} = \alpha_i + X'_{it}\,\delta + Z'_i\,\gamma + v_{it}, \tag{4}$$

where $i = 1, \ldots, N$ and $t = 1,\ldots, T$. The Z_i are individual time-invariant regressors, whereas the X_{it} are time-varying. α_i is assumed to be i.i.d.$(0, \sigma^2_\alpha)$ and v_{it} i.i.d.$(0, \sigma^2_v)$, both independent of each other. The matrices X and Z can be split into two sets of variables $X=[X_1, X_2]$ and $Z=[Z_1, Z_2]$, such that X_1 is $NT \times k_1$, X_2 is $NT \times k_2$, Z_1 is $NT \times g_1$, and Z_2 is $NT \times g_2$. The X_1 and Z_1 are assumed exogenous and not correlated with α_i and v_{it}, while X_2 and Z_2 are endogenous due to their correlation with α_i but not with v_{it}. Hausman & Taylor (1981) suggest an instrumental variables estimator which pre-multiplies expression (4) by $\Omega^{-1/2}$, where Ω is the variance- covariance term of the error component $\alpha_i + v_{it}$, and then performing 2SLS using $[Q, X_1, Z_1]$ as instruments. Q is the within transformation matrix with $X^* = QX$ having a typical element $X^*_{it} = X_{it} - \bar{X}_i$ and $\bar{X}_i$ is the individual mean. This is equivalent to running 2SLS with $[X^*, X_1, Z_1]$ as the set of instruments. If the model is identified, in the sense that there are at least as many time-varying exogenous regressors X_1 as there are individual time-invariant endogenous regressors Z_2, i.e. $k_1 \geq g_2$, this Hausman-Taylor estimator is more efficient than fixed effects. If the model is under-identified, i.e. $k_1 < g_2$, then one cannot estimate γ and the Hausman-Taylor estimator of δ is identical to fixed effects (Hausman & Taylor, 1981; Wooldridge, 2002).

In the case under consideration, education is a potentially endogenous, time-invariant regressor, whereas the experience variables may also be endogenous, but time-varying. Since we are interested in the coefficients of these variables, all the exogenous variables (either time-invariant or time-varying), plus the individual means over time of all the time-varying regressors can be used as instruments to obtain consistent estimates of the returns to education and experience. These instruments are chosen based on Hausman specification tests (Hausman, 1978) in a sequential procedure according to (Baltagi et al., 2003). Specifically, a first Hausman test is the standard to distinguish between the random and fixed effects estimators. A second Hausman test contrasts the Hausman-Taylor against the fixed effects model. Although the fixed effects estimator is not an option in our study, since it does not allow for the estimation of the coefficients of the time invariant regressors, it is useful in order to test the strict exogeneity of the regressors used as instruments in the Hausman-Taylor estimation. Thus, when strict exogeneity for a set of regressors is rejected, others must be considered in the estimation to act as instruments. Once the second Hausman test has identified the regressors that are strictly exogenous, they are used as instruments in the Hausman-Taylor estimation. Additionally, the variance-covariance structure can be taken into account to obtain more efficient estimators (Im et al., 1999), so that the Hausman-Taylor procedure is a good alternative to pure IV estimation when panel data is available.

4. The data and descriptive statistics

The data used in this study come from the ECHP for the period 1994-2000. As stated earlier, this is the only database that provides individual information that is comparable for all EU countries, since the design and organization of the survey is coordinated by EUROSTAT. Individual or micro data is preferred to more aggregate data, both because they provide more flexibility in creating sample restrictions, and because they allow us to directly control for individual-level characteristics in our regression.

At the time of the interview, individuals are requested to indicate whether they are working in a job for at least 15 hours a week. If so, workers identify themselves as either self-employed or employed when asked about their main labor market activity (paid apprenticeships and unpaid work in a family enterprise are excluded from the analysis). As a consequence, the job status of a particular worker may vary from year to year. In the sample, we have selected those workers, either self-employed or wage earners, who have provided information for all variables under consideration. These variables include personal and labor characteristics such as gender, marital status, schooling, experience, earnings, seniority, occupation, whether the individual works in the private or in the public sector, the number of hours worked per week, and if the worker has taken some training course during the last year.

Table 2 illustrates the main characteristics of our samples for the three countries. The number corresponding to wage earners in the sample ranges from about 6,500 in the UK to

more than 8,000 in Germany. For the self-employed, the figures are considerably lower, varying between less than 1,000 in Germany to almost 2,500 in Italy. Sample proportions are not very different from population rates (see Table 1). Bearing in mind that self-employed earnings are commonly believed to be under-reported (Hamilton, 2000), wage earners appear to earn a little more than the self-employed in Italy, whereas the opposite occurs in Germany and in the UK. Note that dispersion in earnings is higher for the self-employed, reflecting a greater heterogeneity in these types of activities, from low-ability jobs (retailers and basic services) to those of professionals, such as doctors or lawyers. People living in Germany and in the UK obtain higher earnings than those residing in Italy.
The years of experience are clearly higher in the self-employed sector than in that of wage earners. The majority of individuals in Italy present low educational levels, the percentage being somewhat higher among the self-employed. By contrast, in Germany, workers in general are highly educated, with more than 40% of the self-employed having attained a tertiary degree. The case of the UK is especially appealing since workers attaining a secondary level are clearly fewer than those of primary or higher education, indicating some kind of a bi-modal distribution. Roughly speaking, where self-employment rates are higher, the self-employed themselves are less educated, as against countries with low self-employment rates, which exhibit a higher proportion of workers, either wage earners or the self-employed, who have obtained at least a secondary level of education.

		Earnings per hour	Exp.	Primary educ.	Secondary educ.	Higher educ.	Obs. per year
Germany	Self-employed	9.06 (8.26)	22.94 (10.98)	12.31	46.19	41.50	840
	Wage earner	8.48 (4.30)	20.48 (11.16)	19.48	57.88	22.64	8066
Italy	Self-employed	6.21 (5.31)	23.69 (13.34)	56.82	31.95	11.23	2494
	Wage earner	6.73 (3.55)	18.03 (11.07)	44.13	44.63	11.24	7865
United Kingdom	Self-employed	8.71 (9.73)	25.33 (13.03)	46.48	13.74	39.78	1053
	Wage earner	7.88 (5.59)	20.02 (12.86)	45.99	13.70	40.31	6433

Table 2. Sample averages (ECHP 1994-2000). Note: Standard errors between parentheses. Earnings are expressed in terms of the PPP. Observations per year is the average, since figures vary from year to year.

5. Estimation results

This section presents the empirical evidence which is then assessed in the light of the aspects mentioned in Section 2, with the aim of providing some insights into the functioning of the European labour markets. The results from EGIV Hausman-Taylor estimations are shown in Table 3, along with the tests for choosing the appropriate instruments (Baltagi et al., 2003). In column H1, a standard Hausman test rejects the random effects hypotheses in favour of the fixed effect estimator. A second Hausman test contrasting the Hausman-Taylor against the fixed effects model (column H2), is useful in order to test the strict exogeneity of the regressors used as instruments in the Hausman-Taylor estimation. Once this second Hausman test has identified which regressors are strictly exogenous, they are then used as instruments in the Hausman-Taylor estimation.

Comparing the coefficients of Table 3 with those from the GLS estimation (not shown, but available from the authors upon request), we can note that the Hausman-Taylor estimation provides coefficients of education and experience that, in general, are consistently much higher. This is in accordance with the typical finding reported in the literature when using instrumental variables of upward bias in IV-type, compared to OLS-type estimations.

Regarding the returns to education, wages increase with educational attainment, with returns higher among wage earners in Germany and Italy and quite similar in the UK, and the coefficients for the self-employed with secondary education level in Germany and the UK are non-significant. The percentage changes across educational categories, computed as the difference in the percentage change in wage for group i relative to the group i-1, $e^{\beta_i}- e^{\beta_{i-1}}$, where β_i is the coefficient for the dummy variable for group I, show that returns increase as we move up the qualification ladder, especially from secondary to higher education, which supports a convex configuration of earnings on the returns to education, thus confirming the importance of the sheepskin effect. Both results, higher returns to education for paid workers, and increasing non-linearities in the relationship between wages and educational attainment, indicate some degree of a sorting or signalling role played by education.

Country	Labour status	Exp.	Exp.^{2}/100	Second. education	Higher education	H1	H2
Germany	Self-employed	0.053**	-0.068**	0.654	1.243*	234.96	8.44
		(3.72)	(-2.83)	(0.89)	(2.45)	(0.0000)	(0.9986)
	Wage earners	0.065**	-0.084**	0.848**	1.291**	1117.89	10.51
		(22.24)	(-22.21)	(8.83)	(17.31)	(0.0000)	(0.9921)
Italy	Self-employed	0.037**	-0.053**	0.339**	0.631**	138.47	34.66
		(6.30)	(-4.66)	(2.78)	(6.35)	(0.0000)	(0.0946)
	Wage earners	0.047**	-0.089**	0.551**	0.847**	2103.26	49.63
		(27.52)	(-23.60)	(15.09)	(19.07)	(0.0000)	(0.0752)
United Kingdom	Self-employed	0.053**	-0.055**	0.629	0.714**	275.90	5.92
		(5.16)	(-3.41)	(0.74)	(3.54)	(0.0000)	(0.9999)
	Wage earners	0.063**	-0.106**	0.524**	0.706**	2064.11	4.58
		(27.27)	(-27.28)	(3.41)	(15.14)	(0.0000)	(1.0000)

Table 3 Estimated Coefficients of Mincerian Earnings Function by Hausman-Taylor. Notes: t-ratios between parentheses (p-values in H1 and H2). Both panels are unbalanced, since the employment status may vary across individuals over time. Controls used. Gender: 1 for male and 0 for female. Marital status: married, single, divorced, widow or separated. Training: if the worker has realized some course of occupational training. Eight dummies that indicate occupation. A dummy indicating whether the individual works in the private or the public sector. Dummies that indicate seniority: less than two years, between 2 and 10 years, and more than 10 years. Dummies that indicate the year. * Significant at the 5% level. ** Significant at the 1% level. H1 tests the random effects estimator against the fixed effects. H2 tests the Hausman-Taylor estimator against the fixed effects.

Across countries, experience increases human capital accumulation during the life cycle. At first sight, returns to experience are greater for wage earners, even though they depreciate at a faster rate than in the case of the self-employed. In order to extract more robust conclusions, a series of indicators are used. First, the maximum return, i.e. the point where experience ceases to add positively to earnings, which is defined by $\partial \ln w / \partial Exp$ from earnings equation (3), that is to say, the number of years that equals $\mu_1 + \mu_2$ Exp/50 to 0 provided $\mu_2 < 0$. The third column in Table 4 is viewed as always being greater for the self-employed, but with marked differences across countries. Thus, the maximum number of years is almost equal in Germany, close to 39 years, with differences around ten years in Italy and almost 20 in the UK. In this latter case, experience is continually adding to earnings during the whole working life of the self-employed. The effects of experience are less long-lasting in Italy, especially among wage earners.

Country	Labour Status	Maximum rate	At sample average
Germany	Self-employed	39	2,18
	Wage earner	38,7	2,36
Italy	Self-employed	35	1,61
	Wage earner	26	1,49
United Kingdom	Self-employed	48	2,51
	Wage earner	30	2,06

Table 4. Returns to experience. Note: Own calculations from the estimated coefficients obtained in Tables 3.

We have computed the series of rates of return as $\mu_1 + \mu_2$ Exp/50, with "Exp" playing the role of a variable. Column 4 in Table 4 reports the rate of return evaluated at the sample average in each country. Values are quite similar in Germany and the UK, and clearly lower in Italy. The greatest difference between the self-employed and wage earners is found in the UK, close to 0.5.

Earnings-experience profiles are constructed from the series of rates of return to experience. Figure 1 displays these profiles for both types of workers in the sample countries. It is clear from the evidence that the profiles are very similar during the first years, (14 in Italy, around 20 in the UK and almost 38 in Germany), with the profiles being slightly steeper for wage earners; then the profiles switch position, revealing the long-lasting effects of experience for the self-employed.

Overall, the body of evidence seems to indicate that investment considerations may be at work, al least in the long run. This can be due to the fact that returns to other capital accumulation, physical or technological, are more long-lasting than those from human capital alone. Alternatively, it can be argued that, if mobility costs are reduced, only well-matched self-employed workers remain as such, with less successful entrepreneurs leaving self-employment and undertaking paid employment. Taken together, it may be reasoned that competitive functioning of the labour market may be at work in these countries. While the different theories cannot be compared one with another in the absence of a more detailed analysis, it nevertheless appears that imperfections in the labour market play a less important role than expected.

In summary, as regards the functioning of the labour market in the set of EU countries considered in this Chapter, two basic ideas emerge. First, returns to education are, in

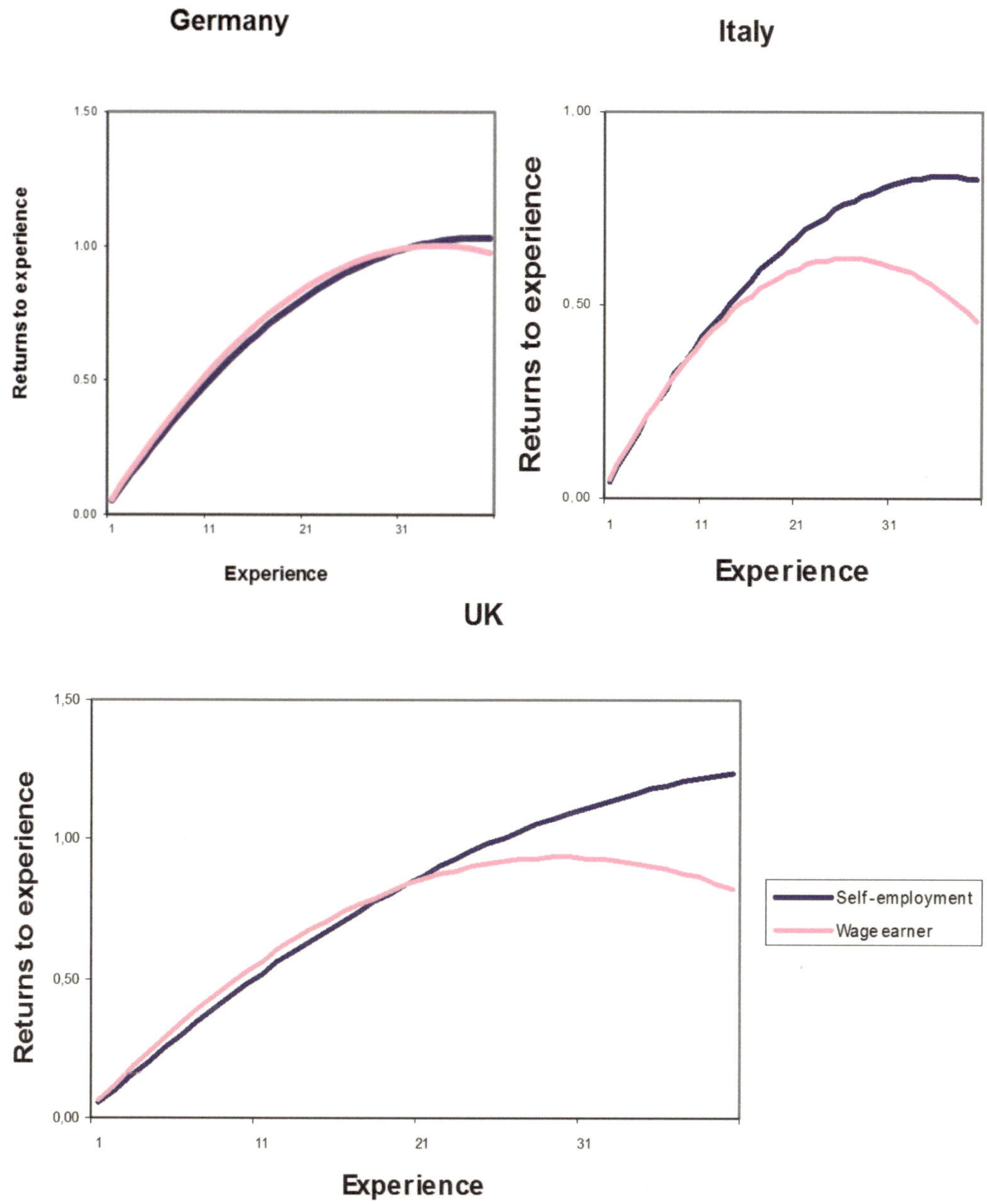

Fig. 1. Earnings experience profiles for the three sample countries

general, found to be higher for wage earners, which can be interpreted as an indication of the relevance of the signalling role of education in determining earnings. This latter result was expected, bearing in mind the prevalent wage rates in the EU countries, where earnings are usually linked to the education level attained by the worker. Second, according to the evidence shown by the earning-experience profiles, which tend to be steeper in the case of the self-employed, traits of competitiveness can be discerned, with little or no evidence of imperfections.

6. Conclusions

The aim of this Chapter has been to extend the existing research on the returns to human capital accumulation that differentiates between the self-employed and wage earners. This has been carried out by providing evidence in a cross-country framework using a homogenous database, which mitigates the problems associated with the existence of different data sources across countries, by using a panel data approach that is useful in dealing with endogeneity and selectivity biases, as well as unobserved heterogeneity, and by applying an efficient estimation method that allows for the correlation between individual effects and time-invariant regressors, and that avoids the insecurity associated with the choice of the appropriate instruments.

Information from the ECHP for the period 1994-2000 has been used, allowing us to apply an Efficient Generalised Instrumental Variable estimator that provides consistent estimates of the rates of return to education and experience. Education has been represented by dummies of qualification levels (primary, secondary and higher), and experience has been measured as the difference between the current age and the age of initiation at work. The results have been presented in a reduced form, with the aim being to provide both comparisons across countries about the earnings differentials between the two employment statuses analyzed, and evidence as to whether such differences are consistent with the predictions offered by a variety of theoretical models.

The self-employed have been used as a control group to help in assessing the true impact of credentials achieved in the process of wage determination, as well as in determining which type of theoretical structure underlies labour market behavior. We have operated under the premise that, on the basis that signalling is of much less importance for the self-employed, comparing across both types of employment statuses should show that, for the sorting hypothesis to be accepted, returns to education for wage earners are significantly higher than those for the self-employed, as well as possibly increasing in a non-linear way. Similarly, most labour market models based on imperfect information predict steeper experience-earnings profiles for wage earners, whereas competitive traits in the labor market would imply similar or flatter profiles for this category of worker.

The evidence that emerges for the sample countries tends to support the view that signalling theory is indeed relevant in determining individual earnings, in that, first, returns to education are lower where signalling is expected to play a less important role, i.e. in the case of the self-employed, and, second, certain non-linearities appear. Furthermore, earnings-experience profiles are found to be steeper for the self-employed in the long-run, indicating a certain significance of competitiveness in the labour markets.

Some aspects of the investigation have been omitted or require further attention. We are conscious that selectivity issues should be carefully dealt with, when the development of a reliable instrument makes this possible (Semykina & Wooldridge, 2010). Furthermore, obtaining structural estimates for the returns to education and experience would probably require dynamic programming models of occupational choice (Belzil & Hansen, 2002). Finally, the availability of richer panel data sets is of particular importance to control for the movements into and out of self-employment. These topics are all matters for future research, and will undoubtedly be helpful in carrying out a more in-depth investigation into the behaviour of the labour market and wage determination in the EU countries, in such a way that we can more fully assess their degrees of competitiveness.

7. Acknowledgements

We are grateful to Adriaan Kalwij for his useful comments and suggestions. We also wish to acknowledge the financial support provided by the Spanish Ministry of Science and Innovation, Project ECO2008-01297.

8. References

Angrist, J. & Krueger, A (1991). Does Compulsory Schooling Attendance Affect Schooling and Earnings? *Quarterly Journal of Economics,* Vol. 106 (November 1991), pp. 979-1014, ISSN 0033-5533.

Angrist, J. & Krueger, A (1999). Empirical Strategies in Labor Economics. In *Handbook of Labor Economics,* 3A, O. Ashenfelter & D. Card (Eds.), pp. 1277-1366, Elsevier Science, ISBN 978-044-4534-68-2, Amsterdam, The Netherlands.

Ashenfelter, O. & Krueger, A. (1994). Estimates of the Economic Return to Schooling from a New Sample of Twins. *American Economic Review,* Vol.84, (December 1994), pp. 1157-1173, ISSN 0002-8282.

Ashenfelter, O.; Harmon, C. & Oosterbeek, H. (1999). A Review of Estimates of the Schooling/Earnings Relationship, with Tests for Publication Bias. *Labour Economics,* Vol.6 (November 1999), pp. 453-470, ISSN 0927-5371.

Baltagi, B.; Bresson, G. & Pirotte, A. (2003). Fixed Effects, Random Effects or Hausman-Taylor? A Pretest Estimator. *Economics Letters* Vol.79 (June 2003), pp. 361-369, ISSN 0165-1765.

Becker, G. (1962). Investment in human capital: A theoretical analysis. *Journal of Political Economy,* Vol.70, pp. 9-49, ISSN 0022-3808.

Becker, G. (1964). *Human Capital: A Theoretical and Empirical Analysis, with Special Reference to Education.* National Bureau of Economics Research, ISBN, 978-0226041209, New York, USA.

Belman, D. & Heywood, J. (1991). Sheepskin Effects in the Return to Education. *Review of Economics and Statistics,* Vol.73 (November 1991), pp. 720-724, ISSN 0034-6535.

Belzil, C. & Hansen, J. (2002). Unobserved Ability and the Return to Schooling. *Econometrica,* Vol.70 (September 2002), pp, 2075-2091, ISSN 0012-9682.

Bound, J.; Jaeger, D. & Baker, R. (1995). Problems with Instrumental Variables Estimation When the Correlation Between the Instruments and Endogenous Explanatory Variable Is Weak. *Journal of the American Statistical Association,* Vol.90 (June 1995), pp. 443-450, ISSN 0162-1459.

Card, D. (1995). Using Geographic Variation in College Proximity to Estimate the Return to Schooling." In *Aspects of Labour Market Behaviour: Essays in Honour of John Vanderkamp* L. Christofides, K. Grant & R. Swidinsky (Eds.), pp. 201-22, University of Toronto Press, ISBN 0802028640, Toronto, Canada.

Card, D. (1999). The Causal Effect of Education on Earnings." In *Handbook of Labour Economics,* vol. 3A, O. Ashenfelter & D. Card (Eds.), pp. 1801-1863, Elsevier Science, ISBN 978-044-4534-68-2, Amsterdam, The Netherlands.

Card, D. (2001). Estimating the Returns to Schooling: Progress on Some Persistent Econometric Problems. *Econometrica*, Vol.69 (September 2001), pp. 1127-1160, ISSN 0012-9682.

Chamberlain, G. & Imbens, G. (2004). Random Effects Estimators With Many Instrumental Variables. *Econometrica*, Vol.72 (January 2004), pp. 295-306, ISSN 0012-9682.

Dunn, T. & Holtz-Eakin, D. (2000). Financial Capital, Human Capital, and the Transition to Self-Employment: Evidence from Intergenerational Links. *Journal of Labor Economics*, Vol.18 (April 2000), pp. 282-305, ISSN 0734-306X.

Evans, D. & Jovanovic, B. (1989). An Estimated Model of Entrepreneurial Choice under Liquidity Constraints. *Journal of Political Economy*, Vol.97 (August 1989), pp. 808-27, ISSN 0022-3808.

Evans, D. & Leighton, L. (1989) Some Empirical Aspects of Enterpreneurship. *American Economic Review*, Vol.79 (June 1989), pp. 519-35, ISSN 0002-8282.

Griliches, Z. (1977). Estimating the Returns to Schooling: Some Econometric Problems. *Econometrica*, Vol.45 (January 1977), pp. 1-22, ISSN 0012-9682.

Hamilton, B. (2000). Does Entrepreneurship Pay? An Empirical Analysis of the Returns to Self-Employment. *Journal of Political Economy*, Vol. 108, (June 2000), pp. 604-631, ISSN 0022-3808.

Harmon, C. & Walker, I. (1955). Estimates of the Economic Return to Schooling for the United Kingdom. *American Economic Review*, Vol.85 (December 1995), pp. 1279-1286, , ISSN 0002-8282.

Harmon, C; Oosterbeck, H. & Walker, I. (2003). The Return to Education: Microeconomics. *Journal of Economic Surveys*, Vol.17 (April 2003): 115-155, ISSN 0950-0804.

Hashimoto, M. (1981). Firm-Specific Human Capital as a Shared Investment. *American Economic Review*, Vol.71 (June 1981), pp. 475-482, ISSN 0002-8282.

Hausman, J. (1978). Specification Test in Econometrics. *Econometrica*, Vol.46 (November 1978), pp. 1251-1271, ISSN 0012-9682.

Hausman, J. & Taylor, W. (1981). Panel Data and Unobservable Individual Effects. *Econometrica*, Vol.49 (November 1981), pp. 1377-1398, ISSN 0012-9682.

Hungerford, T. & Solon, G. (1987). Sheepskin Effects in the Return to Education. *Review of Economics and Statistics*, Vol.69 (1987), pp. 176-178, ISSN 0034-6535.

Im, K.; Ahn, S.; Schmidt, P. & Wooldridge, J. (1999). Efficient Estimation of Panel Data Models with Strictly Exogenous Explanatory Variables. *Journal of Econometrics*, Vol.93 (November 1999), pp. 177-201, ISSN 0304-4076.

Jaeger, D. & Page, M. (1996). Degrees Matter: New Evidence on Sheepskin Effects in the Returns to Education. *Review of Economics and Statistics*, Vol.78 (November 1996), pp. 733-40, ISSN 0034-6535.

Jovanovic, B. (1979). Job Matching and the Theory of Turnover. *Journal of Political Economy*, Vol.87 (October 1979), pp- 972-90, ISSN 0022-3808.

Jovanovic, B. (1982). Selection and the Evolution of Industry. *Econometrica*, Vol.50 (May 1982), pp. 649-670, ISSN 0012-9682.

Kawaguchi, D. (2003). Human Capital Accumulation of Salaried and Self-Employed Workers. *Labour Economics*, Vol.10 (February 2003), pp. 55-71, ISSN 0927-5371.

Lazear, E. (1981). Agency, Earnings Profiles, Productivity, and Hours Restrictions. *American Economic Review*, Vol.71 (September 1981), pp. 606-620, ISSN 0002-8282.

Lazear, E. & Moore, R. (1984). Incentives, Productivity, and Labor Contracts. *Quarterly Journal of Economics*, Vol.99 (May 1984), pp. 275-296, ISSN 0033-5533.

Miller, P.; Mulvey, C. & Martin, N. (1995). What do Twin Studies Reveal About the Economic Returns to Education? A Comparison of Australian and U.S. Findings. *American Economic Review*, Vol.85 (June 1995), pp. 586-599, ISSN 0002-8282.

Mincer, J. (1974). *Schooling, Experience and Earnings*. Columbia University Press, ISBN 0-870-14265-8, New York, USA.

Polachek, S. & Kim, M. (1994). Panel Estimates of the Gender Earnings Gap: Individual-Specific Intercept and Individual-Specific Slope Models. *Journal of Econometrics*, Vol.61 (March 1994), pp. 23-42 ISSN 0304-4076.

Psacharopoulos, G. (1973). *Returns to Education: An International Comparison*. Elsevier, Jossey-Bass, San Francisco, USA.

Psacharopoulos, G. (1981). Returns to education: an updated international comparison. *Comparative Education*, Vol.17 (October 1981), pp. 321-341 ISSN 0305-0068.

Psacharopoulos, G. (1985). Returns to Education: A Further International Update and Comparison. *Journal of Human Resources*, Vol.20 (Fall 1985), pp. 583-597 ISSN 0022-166X.

Psacharopoulos, G. (1994). Returns to Investment in Education: A Global Update. *World Development*, Vol.22 (September 1994), pp. 1325-1343 ISSN 0305-750X.

Rees, H. & Shah, A. (1986). An Empirical Analysis of Self-Employment in the UK. *Journal of Applied Econometrics*, Vol.1 (January 1986),pp. 95-108 ISSN 1099-1255.

Riley, J. (1979). Testing the Educational Screening Hypothesis. *Journal of Political Economy*, Vol.87, (October 1979), pp. S227-S251, ISSN 0022-3808.

Rosen, S. (1981). The Economics of Superstars. *American Economic Review*, Vol.71, (December 1981), pp. 845-858, ISSN 0002-8282.

Rosenzweig, M. & Wolpin, K. (2000). Natural "Natural Experiments" in Economics. *Journal of Economics Literature*, Vol.38, (2000), pp. 827-874, ISSN 0022-0515.

Salop, J. & Salop, S. (1976). Self-Selection and Turnover in the Labor Market. *Quarterly Journal of Economics*, Vol.90, (November 1976), pp. 619-627, ISSN 0033-5533.

Semykina, A. & Wooldridge, J. (2010). Estimating Panel Data Models in the Presence of Endogeneity and Selection. *Journal of Econometrics*, Vol.157, (June 2010), pp. 375-380, ISSN 0304-4076.

Spence, M. (1973). Job Market Signaling. *Quarterly Journal of Economics*, Vol.87, (August 1973), 355-374, ISSN 0033-5533.

Staiger, D. & Stock, J. (1997). Instrumental Variables Regressions With Weak Instruments. *Econometrica*, Vol.65 (May 1997), pp. 557-586, ISSN 0012-9682.

Stiglitz, J. (1975). The Theory of Screening, Education and the Distribution of Income. *American Economic Review*, Vol.65, (June 1975), pp. 283-300, ISSN 0002-8282.

Trostel, P.; Walker, I. & Woolley, P. Estimates of the Economic Return to Schooling for 28 Countries. *Labour Economics*, Vol.9, (February 2002), pp. 1-16, ISSN 0927-5371.

Weiss, A. (1995). Human Capital vs. Signalling Explanation of Wages. *Journal of Economic Perspectives*, Vol.9, (Fall 1995), pp. 133-154, ISSN 0895-3309.

Wolpin, K. (1977). Education and Screening. *American Economic Review*, Vol.67, (December 1977), pp. 949-958, ISSN 0002-8282.

Wooldridge, J. (2002). *Econometric Analysis of Cross Section and Panel Data*. MIT Press, ISBN 0-262-23219-7, Cambridge, MA, USA.

6

Using the SUR Model of Tourism Demand for Neighbouring Regions in Sweden and Norway

A. Khalik Salman
Mid Sweden University, Social science / Economics Department
Sweden

1. Introduction

This chapter estimates the international demand for tourism in two neighbouring regions: the objective number 6 (SW:6) in Sweden and North Norway included - Tröndelag (NWT) in North Norway, from five different countries: Denmark, the United Kingdom, Switzerland, Japan, and the United States. For each visiting country, and for Sweden and Norway, we specify separate equations by including the relevant information. we then estimate these ten equations using Zellner's Iterative Seemingly Unrelated Regressions (ISUR). The benefit of this model is that the ISUR estimators utilize the information within and the relation between the equations present in the error correlation of the cross regressions (or equations) and hence is more efficient than single equation estimation methods such as ordinary least squares. Monthly time series data from 1993:01 to 2006:12 are used. The results show that the consumer price index, some lagged dependent variables, and several monthly dummies (representing seasonal effects) have significant impacts on the number of visitors to the SW:6 region in Sweden and NWT region in Norway. We also find that, in at least some cases, relative prices and exchange rates have significant effects on international tourism demand.

Tourism has important impacts on the economies of both developing and industrialized countries, resulting in job creation, additional income for the private and public sectors, foreign currency receipts, higher investment and growth. Indeed, tourism has acted as a catalyst to economic restructuring in many recipient countries, assisting a shift away from primary sector activities, towards greater reliance on services and manufacturing. Given the scale of tourism's contribution to the macroeconomic dimension over time, knowledge concerning the nature of the demand upon which it is based is of both theoretical and practical relevance. It is well known that tourism demand is responsive to such variables as income, relative prices and exchange rates. What is not known is how the responsiveness of demand to changes in these variables alters during a country's economic transition and integration into the wider world initial or subsequent years? Does the sensitivity of tourism demand to changes in its own prices, or those of its competitors, change between different periods? Further questions concern the degrees of complementarity or substitutability between tourism destinations and the extent to which these change during periods of economic transition. Complementarity occurs if holidays in different destinations are purchased as a package. Alternatively, there may be an intense degree of competition between destinations. Relationships of complementarity or substitutability may change over time as lower income destinations emerge from relative poverty to achieve a higher level of development. Little information is available about this issue. It is not known, for example, whether lower income destinations tend to become more or less competitive over time, either relative to other developing countries or relative to more industrialized nations.

Different models have been used to estimate tourism demand and some types of model are more appropriate for examining the above questions than others. The vast majority of studies of tourism demand have relied on single equation models of demand, estimated within a static context (for example, Uysal and Crompton, 1984; Gunadhi and Boey,1986). These models are not derived from consumer demand theory and fail to quantify the changes in demand behaviour that occur over time. Innovations in the methodology were subsequently introduced in the form of single equation models of demand estimated using an error correction methodology were subsequently introduced in single equation model of demand estimated using an error correction methodology (Syriopoulos, 1995). Kulendran (1996) used a general to specific, error correction model to estimate the Australia demand for tourism in the form of visits per capita to outbound destinations and demonstrated that the model has good forecasting ability. This modelling approach has the advantage of explicit treatment of the time dimension of tourism demand behaviour and allows for improved econometric estimation of the specified equations.

A More recently approach to tourism demand estimation involves a system -wide approach by using the ISUR Model (Salman et al. 2010). This system of study is particularly useful for testing the properties of homogeneity and symmetry which are basic to consumer demand theory. Hence, it provides a stronger theoretical basic for estimating the cross- price elasticities of demand than the single equation approach.

This chapter was used system wise approach by the ISUR Model to examine tourism demand by the UK, Switzerland, Denmark, Japan and The USA in the neighboring destination number 6 (SW:6) and (NWT) in Norway. The UK, Switzerland, Denmark, Japan and The USA are major origin countries for tourism in the destinations under consideration. SW:6 in Sweden and NWT in Norway are key destinations, accounting for over one-third of all receipts from tourism in the European Union in 2005. The absolute value of their receipts from tourism is very high, at over $ 200 million in 2005. The choice of the countries as destinations for analysis is also appropriate owing to their position as geographic neighbours. Complementarity or substitutability in tourism demand, as indicated by the signs of the relative-price elasticities of demand, is of particular relevance in this context. This chapter pays attention to this issue, which has not previously been examined for the case of neighbouring countries using the ISUR approach. Sweden and Norway are interesting cases for consideration owing to their position as economies in transition during the period under consideration. By the early 1990s, the start years of the period under study, they had adopted new development policies, high dependence on industry, moving towards increased globalization, economic integration, and foreign competition. Sweden had joined the ranks of the more developed European economies in the period under study. Hence, an innovative feature of this chapter is its examination of the evolution of tourism demand during these countries' transition to a new technological system and globalization status. It also permits examination of the extent to which the behaviour of demand become more or less similar over time with respect to changes in prices and exchange rates. Thus, this study provides useful information, at the cross-country level, about change in a major activity within each of the economies.

The aim of this chapter is to estimate international tourism demand to the two neighbouring regions: objective number 6 (SW:6) in Sweden and North Norway included - Tröndelag

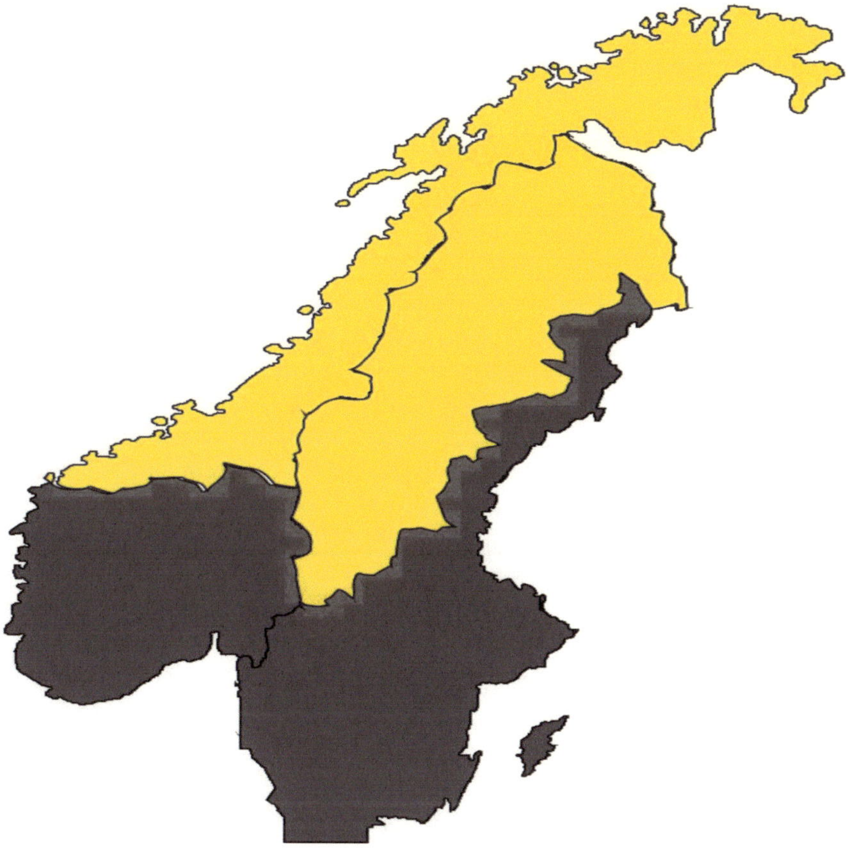

Fig. 1. Swedish and Norwegian Maps; The Objective 6 region (SW: 6) in Sweden is the lightly shadowed area at the top and top-left of the map of Sweden. The North -Norway included and Tröndelag region in Norway (NWT) is the lightly shadowed part on the top right of the map of Norway.

(NWT) by five countries: namely, Denmark, the United Kingdom (UK), Switzerland, Japan, and the United States (US). Since these two regions are geographically very close to each others and highly competitive (although they are located in two different countries) we believe that they can be considered as one larger region with respect to the very similar nature and tourism facilities they supply. For this reason we study the demand for these two regions simultaneously together by specifying a separate equation for these regions from the respective visiting countries. We then merge the ten equations in one system of regression equations model that will be estimated by Zellner's ISUR model.
Previous Scandinavian studies did not study and compare the tourism demand for Sweden and Norway in one overall regression model. Further, previous studies of Norwegian tourism demand have not considered the relative price and substitution effect or complementarity, the real and nominal exchange rate, and personal income. With this method of estimation, I can

come closer to studying the impact of the influences of cultural values, climate natural attraction on the tourism demand. This has earlier been difficult to quantify.

The purpose of this chapter is to use Iterative Seemingly Unrelated Regressions (ISUR) to estimate the relationship between monthly tourist arrivals to Sweden and Norway from Denmark, the UK, Switzerland, Japan, and the US and the factors that influence arrivals. To this end, we use a demand function approach to tourism flow modelling. A large model consisting of ten equations for Sweden and Norway (five for each country) was estimated by the ISUR technique.

The idea of merging the equations from both countries into one overall model, in fact, is necessary to measure the tourism demand to neighbouring regions that are close in their geographical characters, see Figure 1. In other words, tourists can receive the same utility from either region. An important question is "Are there differences between the hedonic regressions for the two neighbourhoods, or not?" If there are no differences, then the data from the two neighbourhoods can be pooled into one sample without parameter restrictions and with no allowance made for differing slope or intercept. Moreover, the estimation has been done by using the ISUR regression.

There is no previous application of this technique to tourism demand modelling for these two regions. With the ISUR technique, we estimate the entire system of equations by taking into account any possible correlations between the residuals from the different equations. Moreover, the ISUR technique provides parameter estimates that converge to unique maximum likelihood parameter estimates.

The remainder of the chapter is organized as follows. Section 2 discusses tourism demand for Nordic countries and the data used. Section 3 presents the estimation and testing methodology. Section 4 provides the results. This chapter has a brief summary and conclusion in Section 5.

2. Economic factors and the model specification

The objective of this section is to analyze how the following macroeconomic and microeconomic variables and seasonal (monthly) conditions influence the demand for tourism for the (SW:6) and (NWT):

1. The Swedish Consumer Price Index (CPI) represents the inflation rate and cost of living in Sweden and is in natural logarithms. The CPI has several advantages for this purpose: it is familiar to the public and is the most widely used measure of inflation in Sweden (Andersson and Berg, 1995). We adjust the CPI for any changes in indirect taxes and subsidies.
2. I use dummy variables for January to November to proxy for seasonal effects (December is the base category).
3. The exchange rate (*EX*) between the Swedish/Norwegian currencies and the visitors' country of origin currency are included in natural logarithms.
4. The relative price (*Pr*) reflects opportunity cost. This represents the cost of living in relative terms for Norway and Sweden and a substitute price for an origin country tourist. These are also in natural logarithms.

The SW:6 is a major tourist destination worldwide, with the yearly demand for tourism in this part of Sweden and NWT consistently following an upward trend. However, interruption to these trends has taken place on a number of occasions due to economic conditions and/or international events. For example, September 11 and the first Gulf War had a detrimental effect on tourism demand in both Sweden and Norway.

A common model used in tourism demand studies is a single equation with demand explained by the tourist's income in their country of origin, the cost of tourism in their chosen and alternative destinations, and a substitute price (Witt and Martin, 1987). To start with, the demand for tourism can be expressed in a variety of ways. The most appropriate variable to represent demand explained by economic factors is consumer expenditure or receipts (Grouch, 1992). Other measures of demand are the nights spent by the tourist or their length of stay. However, due to the lack of data on monthly GDP, personal income (GDP/Population) is not included in this analysis.

The tourism price index (the price of the holiday) is also an important determinant of the decision a potential tourist makes. We can divide this into two components: (i) the cost of living for the tourist at the destination, and (ii) the cost of travel or transport to the destination. I divide the cost of living into two components: (i) the CPI in relative price form assuming that tourists have the option of spending their vacation in either SW:6 or NWT, and (ii) tourist consumer expenditure, real consumer expenditure, real income, and per capita income (Salman, 2003). In this chapter, CPI represents the cost of living. However, we measure transport costs by the weighted mean prices according to the transport mode used by tourists to reach the destination. Changes in travel costs, particularly airfares, can have a major impact on tourism demand. Unfortunately, data on economy class airfares between Stockholm and the capital cities of the countries of origin were not consistently available, so I could not use these in construction of the variables. Moreover, one should also take into account the small proportion of tourists who arrive in Sweden using charter flights destined for regional airports closer to the main tourist resorts, as the airfares for these may differ considerably from those to the capital city's airport. Therefore, in the absence of a suitable proxy, I exclude travel costs from our demand system (Lathiras and Siriopoulos, 1998).

In previous Scandinavian tourism demand studies, the cost of living component was defined in relative price form, assuming that the tourists have the option of spending their vacation in Sweden or at home. The probability of travel to the destination declines if the destination price level increased faster than that of the origin price due to a substitution effect, and also if the if the reserves occurred and hence the tourist's real income decreased to the substitution effect .

In this study, the cost of living (relative price) component is defined as the Norwegian price relative to the price of a holiday in Sweden. The underlying assumption is that for the tourists, SW: -6 in Sweden is a substitute long-haul holiday destination for NWT in Norway. In recent years, SW:6 in Sweden and NWT in Norway have been competing with each other to attractive more tourists. The tourists from these five countries have the option of spending vacations on SW:6 in Sweden or NWT in Norway, both having similar mountains and skiing facilities in winter and similar climate. Furthermore, for visitors from these five countries mentioned above, the travel distances to SW:- 6 in Sweden and NWT in Norway are almost the same. Therefore, for potential visitors, SW:6 is consider a substitute long-haul holiday destination for the NWT and the cost of living variable for the tourism demand model is defined as the cost of living in SW:6 relative to that for NWT in Norway .

Following previous research, we can specify the price of tourism at the destination in a variety of ways. For instance, we can represent prices in either absolute or relative terms. In this chapter, we employ the relative price as an opportunity cost. We define this as the ratio of the CPI of the host country (CPI_{SW}) to the country of origin adjusted by the relative exchange rate (R_{it}) to obtain a proxy for the real cost of living (Salman, 2004). Therefore, the real cost of tourism in Sweden and Norway are the relative CPIs given by:

$$Rp_{jt} = \frac{\dfrac{\mathrm{CPI}_{it}}{EX_{ijt}}}{\mathrm{CPI}_{jt}} \tag{1}$$

where i is the host country (Sweden or Norway), j is the visiting (or foreign) country, and t is time. Rp_{it} is the relative CPI for country i in time t, CPI_{it} is the CPI for Sweden or Norway, CPI_{jt} is the CPI for the foreign country, and EX_{ijt} is the exchange rate between the Swedish krona/Norwegian krone and the foreign currency.

In addition to the price variable, the exchange rate is a relevant factor in determining tourism demand. The rationale behind incorporation of the exchange rate as a separate explanatory variable is that tourists may be more aware of the relative exchange rate than the specific cost of tourism at the destination. A question that arises is whether the exchange rate should be included in our model system as an explanatory variable together with the price variable. In an attempt to find a variable to represent a tourist's cost of living, Salman, Shukur, and Bergmann-Winberg (2007) concluded that the CPI (either alone or with the exchange rate) is a reasonable proxy of the cost of tourism. And also the exchange rate and price are used in this study as proxy variables for the structural transformation in these two small open economies and the expansion in international competitions faced by them. We define the exchange rate variable as the foreign exchange rate of the Swedish Krona or Norwegian Krona to the currency of the origin country. This variable represents the relationship between tourism demand and the international money market and international economic events (including recessions and financial crises) as well.

As microeconomic theory suggests, the price of other goods influences the demand for a particular good. In the case of tourism, the identification and separation of substitute products is very difficult to achieve on an a priori basis. In our case, tourists consider NWT region (in the North of Norway) an alternative destination to the SW:6 region (in the north of Sweden). These destinations are among the most popular destinations in Scandinavia, at least in terms of arrivals, for tourists from the origin countries under:

Relative price of tourism for Denmark

$$= \frac{CPI_{SweK} / EX_{SEK/DKK}}{CPI_{Nor} / EX_{NOK/DKK}} \tag{2}$$

Relative price of tourism for the UK

$$= \frac{CPI_{Swe} / EX_{SEK/GBP}}{CPI_{Nor} / EX_{NOK/GBP}} \tag{3}$$

Relative price of tourism for Switzerland

$$= \frac{CPI_{Swe} / EX_{SEK/CHF}}{CPI_{Nor} / EX_{NOK/CHF}} \tag{4}$$

Relative price of tourism for Japan

$$= \frac{CPI_{Swe} / EX_{SEK/JPY}}{CPI_{Nor} / EX_{NOK/JPY}} \tag{5}$$

Relative price of tourism for the US

$$= \frac{CPI_{Swe} / EX_{SEK/USD}}{CPI_{Nor} / EX_{NOK/USD}} \tag{6}$$

Where:
CPI_{Swe}: CPI in Sweden (1998 = 100).
$CPINor$: CPI in Norway (1998 = 100).
$EX_{SEK/DKK}$: An index of the Swedish krona per unit of Danish krona (1998 = 100).
$EX_{SEK/GBP}$: An index of the Swedish krona per unit of British pound (1998 = 100).
$EX_{SEK/CHF}$: An index of the Swedish krona per unit of Swiss franc (1998 = 100).
$EX_{SEK/JPY}$: An index of the Swedish krona per unit of Japanese yen (1998 = 100).
$EX_{SEK/USD}$: An index of the Swedish krona per unit of US dollar (1998 = 100).
A lagged dependent variable may also be included to account for habit persistence and supply constraints. As for the signs of the explanatory variables, we expect a negative sign for the relative price variable and a positive sign for the exchange rate variable. In this study, monthly dummies represent seasonal effects on the number of arrivals from the origin countries. All variables are in natural logarithms, and the data are in index form (1998 = 100). All economic data employed in this study are from Statistics Sweden (Statistiska Centralbyrån) and Statistics Norway (Statistisk SENTRALBYRÅ). Estimation is with the STATA Ver. 10 and EViews Ver. 5.1 statistical program packages. We examine monthly time series data from 1993:01 to 2006:12.

3. Methodology

3.1 Statistical assumptions and the problem of misspecification

In the common stochastic specification of econometric models, the error terms are assumed to be normally distributed with mean zero, constant variance and serially uncorrelated. These assumptions must be tested and verified before one can have any confidence in the estimation results or conduct any specification tests, including standard *t*-tests of parameter significance or tests of theoretical restrictions. Because misspecification testing is a vast area of statistical/econometric methodology, there will only be a brief description of the methods used in this study (in the Appendix) with additional details in the cited references.
The methodology used in this chapter for misspecification testing follows Godfrey (1988) and Shukur (2002). To test for autocorrelation, we apply the F-version of the Breusch (1978) and Godfrey (1978) test. We use White (1980) test (including cross products of the explanatory variables) to test for heteroscedasticity and Ramsey's (1969) RESET test to test for functional misspecification (Ramsey, 1969). We also apply the Engle (1980) Lagrange Multiplier (LM) test for the possible presence of Autoregressive Conditional Heteroscedasticity (ARCH) in the residuals. Finally, we apply the Jarque-Bera (1987) LM test of non-normality to the residuals in model (4).
When building an econometric model, the assumption of parameter consistency is widely used because of the resulting simplicity in estimation and ease of interpretation. However,

in situations where a structural change may have occurred in the generation of the observations, this assumption is obviously inappropriate. Particularly in the field of econometrics where data are not generated under controlled conditions, the problem of ascertaining whether the underlying parameter structure is constant is of paramount interest. However, to test for the stability of the parameters in the models, and in the absence of any prior information regarding possible structural changes, we conduct a cumulative sum (CUSUM) test following Brown et al. (1975). The CUSUM test is in the form of a graph and is based on the cumulative sum of the recursive residuals. Movement in these recursive residuals outside the critical lines is suggestive of coefficient instability.

3.2 The systemic specification

In this chapter, we aim to estimate the number of visitors to Sweden and Norway from five countries (Denmark, the UK, Switzerland, Japan, and the US). For each visiting country and for both Sweden and Norway, we specify a separate equation with the relevant information included in each equation. For this purpose, we follow a simple strategy on how to select an appropriate model by successively examining the adequacy of a properly chosen sequence of models for each country separately using diagnostic tests with known good properties. The methodology used for misspecification testing in this chapter follows Godfrey (1988) and Shukur (2002). We apply their line of reasoning to the problem of autocorrelation, and then extend it to other forms of misspecification. If we subject a model to several specification tests, one or more of the test statistics may be so large (or the p-values so small) that the model is clearly unsatisfactory. At that point, one has either to modify the model or search for an entirely new model.

Our aim is to find a well-behaved model that satisfies the underlying statistical assumptions, which at the same time agrees with aspects of economic theory. Given these equations, we estimate the whole system (consisting of ten equations) using Zellner's ISUR. The ISUR technique provides parameter estimates that converge to unique maximum likelihood parameter estimates. Note that conventional seemingly unrelated regressions (SUR) does not have this property if the numbers of variables differ between the equations, even though it is one of the most successful and efficient methods for estimating SUR. The resulting model has stimulated countless theoretical and empirical results in econometrics and other areas (see Zellner, 1962; Srivastava and Giles, 1987; Chib and Greenberg, 1995). The benefit of this model for us is that the ISUR estimators utilize the information present in the cross regression (or equations) error correlation and hence it is more efficient than other estimation methods such as ordinary least squares (OLS).

Consider a general system of m stochastic equations given by:

$$\mathbf{Y}_i = \mathbf{X}_i B_i + e_i \quad i = 1, 2, \ldots \mathrm{M} \tag{7}$$

where $\mathbf{Y}_i$ is a $(T \times 1)$ vector of dependent variables, e_i is a $(T \times 1)$ vector of random errors with $E(e_i) = 0$, $\mathbf{X}_i$ is a $(T \times n_i)$ matrix of observations on n_i exogenous and lagged dependent variables including a constant term, B_i is a $(n_i \times 1)$ dimensional vector of coefficients to be estimated, M is the number of equations in the system, T is the number of observations per equation, and n_i is the number of rows in the vector B_i. The m system of m equations can be written separately as:

$$Y_1 = X_1 \beta_1 + e_1$$

$$Y_2 = X_2\beta_2 + e_2$$

$$Y_m = X_m\beta_m + e_m$$

and then combined into a larger model written as:

$$\begin{pmatrix} Y_1 \\ Y_2 \\ \cdots \\ Y_m \end{pmatrix} = \begin{pmatrix} X_1 & 0 & 0 & 0 \\ 0 & X_2 & 0 & 0 \\ 0 & 0 & \cdots & 0 \\ 0 & 0 & 0 & X_m \end{pmatrix} \cdot \begin{pmatrix} \beta_1 \\ \beta_2 \\ \cdots \\ \beta_m \end{pmatrix} + \begin{pmatrix} e_1 \\ e_2 \\ \cdots \\ e_m \end{pmatrix} \tag{8}$$

This model can be rewritten compactly as:

$$\mathbf{Y} = \mathbf{X}B + e \tag{9}$$

where Y and e are of dimension $(TM \times 1)$, X is of dimension $(TM \times n)$, $n = \sum_{i=1}^{M} n_i$, and B is of dimension $(K \times 1)$.

At this stage, I make the following assumptions:

a. $\mathbf{X}_i$ is fixed with rank n_i.

b. $P\lim \frac{1}{T}(X_i^{'}X_i) = Q_{ii}$ is nonsingular with finite and fixed elements, i.e. invertible.

c. addition, I assume that $P\lim \frac{1}{T}(X_i^{'}X_j) = Q_{ij}$ is also nonsingular with finite and fixed elements.

d. $E(e_i e_i^{'}) = \sigma_{ij} I_T$, where σ_{ij} designates the covariance between the ith and j^{th} equations for each observation in the sample.

The above expression can be written as:

$E(e) = 0$ and $E(ee') = \Sigma \otimes I_T = \Psi$, where $\Sigma = \begin{bmatrix} \sigma_{11} & \sigma_{12} & \cdots & \sigma_{1M} \\ \sigma_{21} & \sigma_{22} & \cdots & \sigma_{2M} \\ \vdots & & \ddots & \\ \sigma_{M1} & \sigma_{M2} & \cdots & \sigma_{MM} \end{bmatrix}$ is an $M \times M$ positive definite symmetric matrix and $\otimes$ is the Kronecker product. Thus, the errors at each equation are assumed homoscedastic and not autocorrelated, but there is contemporaneous correlation between corresponding errors in different equations.

The OLS estimator of B in (9) is:

$$\hat{\beta}_{OLS} = (X'X)^{-1} X'Y$$

with the variance

$$Var(\hat{\beta}_{OLS}) = (X'X)^{-1} X'\Psi X(X'X)^{-1}$$

The SUR Generalized Least Squares (GLS) estimator of B is given by:

$$\hat{\beta}_{GLS} = \left(X'(\Sigma^{-1} \otimes I_T)X\right)^{-1} X'(\Sigma^{-1} \otimes I_T)Y$$

and the variance is given by:

$$V\left(\hat{\beta}_{GLS}\right) = \left(X'(\Sigma^{-1} \otimes I_T)X\right)^{-1}$$

However, the system of the five equations for Sweden and Norway are as follows:

$$Y_{it} = \alpha_i + S_i + X_{it}B_i + Y_{it-q}\Phi_{iq} + e_{it}\,'\, i = 1, 2,\ldots 5 \quad q = 1, 2,\ldots 12 \tag{10}$$

where $\boldsymbol{Y_{it}}$ is a $T \times 1$ vector of observations on the dependent variable, e_{it} is a $T \times 1$ vector of random errors with $E(e_t) = 0$, and S_i are monthly dummy variables that take values between 1 and 11 (the twelfth month is the base). X_{it} is a $T \times n_i$ matrix of observations on n_i nonstochastic explanatory variables, and B_i is an $n_i \times 1$ dimensional vector of unknown location parameters. T is the number of observations per equation, and n_i is the number of rows in the vector B_i. Φ_{iq} is a parameter vector associated with the lagged dependent variable for the respective equation.

The dependent variables $\boldsymbol{Y_i}$ are the natural logarithms of the number of monthly visitors from Denmark, the UK, Switzerland, Japan, and the US to either Sweden or Norway. The matrix X_i is the natural logarithm of three vectors that contains monthly information about the CPI in Sweden (or Norway), the exchange rate (*Ex*) in Sweden (or Norway), and relative price (*Rp*) for Sweden (or Norway) with respect to each of the abovementioned countries.

Another objective of this study is to test for the existence of any contemporaneous correlation between the equations. If such correlation exists and is statistically significant, then least squares applied separately to each equation are not efficient and there is need to employ another estimation method that is more efficient.

The SUR estimators utilize the information present in the cross regression (or equations) error correlation. In this chapter, we estimated the model in Equation (10) by using the OLS method for each equation separately to achieve the best specification of each equation. We then estimate the whole system using ISUR, see Tables 2 and 3. The ISUR technique provides parameter estimates that converge to unique maximum likelihood parameter estimates and take into account any possible contemporaneous correlation between the equations.

To test whether the estimated correlation between these equations is statistically significant, we apply Breusch and Pagan's (1980) LM statistic. If we denote the covariances between the different equations as $\sigma_{12}, \sigma_{13}\ldots\sigma_{45}$, the null hypothesis is:

H_0: $\sigma_{12} = \sigma_{13} \ldots = \sigma_{45} = 0$, against the alternative hypothesis,

H_1: at least one covariance is nonzero.

In our three equations, the test statistic is:

$\lambda = N(r^2_{12} + r^2_{13} + \ldots r^2_{45})$, where r^2_{ij} is the squared correlation,

$r^2_{ij} = \sigma^2_{ij} / \sigma_{ii}\sigma_{jj}$.

Under H_0, λ has an asymptotic χ^2 distribution with five degrees of freedom. I may reject H_0 for a value of λ greater than the critical value from a $\chi^2_{(45)}$ distribution (i.e. with 45 degrees of freedom) for a specified significance level. In this study, the calculated χ^2 value for Sweden and Norway together is equal to 100 (p-value = 0.000). This result, reported in Table 1 below for Sweden and Norway together, suggests a rejection of H_0 at any conventional significance level. This implies that the residuals from each ISUR regressions are significantly positively or negatively correlated with each other that might stand for the relation between these equations and the countries thereafter. Also this can show substitutability and complementarity among destinations by indicating positive and negative correlation of residuals. Clear conclusions about the complementarily or substitutability among destinations are not usually obtained in studies using the correlation matrix of residuals and SUR model.

	Dn/s	UK/s	Swit/s	Jp/s	US/s	Dn/n	UK/n	Swt/n	JP/n	US/n
Dn/s	1.0000									
UK/s	0.0269	1.000								
SWIT/s	0.2497	-0.1475	1.000							
JP/s	-0.0284	0.1550	0.0094	1.000						
US/s	-0.1465	-0.0940	0.1320	0.0389	1.000					
DN/n	-0.0909	0.0829	-0.0716	-0.0579	0.0650	1.000				
UK/n	0.0335	-0.1719	0.1384	-0.0985	-0.0632	-0.0216	1.000			
SWIT/n	0.0876	0.0534	0.0999	-0.0606	0.0350	0.0231	0.1036	1.000		
JP/n	0.0195	-0.0235	0.0236	-0.0828	0.2230	0.1444	-0.0414	0.1493	1.000	
US/n	-0.1943	-0.1549	0.1279	-0.1170	-0.0330	-0.0081	0.3869	-0.0895	-0.0010	1.000

Breusch-Pagan test of independence: chi2(45) = 100, Pr = 0.0000

Table 1. Correlation matrix of residuals for Sweden and Norway:

4. The ISUR results

In this section, we present the most important results from the ISUR method to model international tourism demand to SW:6 in Sweden and NWT in Norway.

We first conduct single equations estimation on model (10) for the five equations for Sweden and the five equations for Norway, separately. We specify these equations according to a battery of diagnostic tests (see the Appendix). We then select the five most appropriate equations for Sweden and Norway and include them separately in ISUR estimation consisting of ten equations to achieve the best possible efficiency. We then discuss the results for each country separately and also compare them together. We first present the results for the three economic variables and then discuss the results for the seasonal dummy variables (with December as the base month), followed by the lagged dependent variables. Note that the macro variables are in logarithmic form and so we can interpret the estimated parameters as elasticities. The estimated coefficients are included even if they are not significant. For the dummy and lagged dependent variables, only coefficients significant at least at the 10% level in the single equation estimation are included in the ISUR estimation.

consisting of ten equations to achieve the best possible efficiency. We then discuss the results for each country separately and also compare them together. We first present the results for the three economic variables and then discuss the results for the seasonal dummy variables (with December as the base month), followed by the lagged dependent variables. Note that the macro variables are in logarithmic form and so we can interpret the estimated parameters as elasticities. The estimated coefficients are included even if they are not significant. For the dummy and lagged dependent variables, only coefficients significant at least at the 10% level in the single equation estimation are included in the ISUR estimation.

Sweden	Equations				
Parameters	Denmark	UK	Switzerland	Japan	US
Constant	.0662(0.974)	-5.732 (0.103)	.879 (0.850)	16.210 (0.000)	1.288 (0.761)
CPI	-. 197 (0.0.024)	2.474 (0.047)	2.474 (0.070)	-6.205 (0.000)	-.1348 (0.688)
EX	1.821 (0.285)	0.782 (0.462)	-1.564 (0.013)	0.1923 (0.456)	0.140 (0.224)
Rp	-.167(0.000)	0.458 (0.000)	-2.250 (.000)	-6.205 (0.004)	-.135 (1.583)
D1	.605 (0.000)	-.367 (.000)			
D2	.638 (0.000)	-.256 (.000)	.1651 (.024)	.1651 (.002)	
D3	.271 (0.069)	-.4119 (.000)	.0887 (.000)		.132 (.007)
D4	-.397 (0.002)	-.432 (.000)	-.195 (.000)	.165 (.107)	-.235 (.000)
D5	-1.04 (0.000)	-.662 (.000)	-.133 (.000)	-.129 (.001)	-.109 (.000)
D6	-.230 (0 .000)	-.063 (.231)	.493 (.000)	.106 (.023)	.343 (.000)
D7	.323 (0 .000)	-.285 (.0000)	.813 (.000)		
D8	-.373 (0.002)	-.385 (.000)	.479 (.000)		
D9	-.788 (0 .000)	-.645 (.000)			-.246 (.000)
D10	-.823 (0.000)	-.486 (.000)	-.343 (.000)		-.251 (.012)
D11	-.894 (0 .000)	-.294 (.000)	.314 (.000)	275 (.083)	-.137 (.000)
Y(t-1)		.6056 (.000)	0.095 (0.082)		
Y(t-2)					
Y(t-3)					
Y(t-4)		-.169 (.001)			
Y(t-11)	.136 (.061)		.116 (.032)	.208 (.000)	.551 (.001)
Y(t-12)	.0411 (.552)	.275 (.000)	.142 (.010)	.594 (.000)	.215 (.063)
R2	0.941	0.900	0.824	0.845	0.742

The non significant results erased from the Table.

Table 2. ISUR estimation results for Sweden

4.1 Results for Sweden

Table 1 show that the CPI parameter for Denmark is negative and small in magnitude but not statistically significant, indicating Swedish CPI has no effect on the demand for tourism by Denmark. This could be due to low travel costs, whereas countries of origin that are more distant generally have higher price elasticity. The estimated *CPISW* elasticity is -6.205 and greater than that for Japan. This indicates that a 1% increase in *CPISW* results in a 6.2% decrease in tourist arrivals to SW6 from Japan. The low *CPISW* elasticity (-0.13) for the US could be a reflection of the depreciation of the Swedish Krona against the US dollar.

The estimated elasticity of the relative (substitute) price ranges from 6.2% to 0.13% and is greater than one for Japan and Switzerland. This indicates that a 1% rise in the relative price level (price of tourism in Sweden relative to Norway) causes more than 1% fall in tourist arrivals from Japan and Switzerland. These estimates indicate that tourist arrivals in Sweden from these countries are elastic with respect to the relative price variable. This implies that Sweden must maintain its international price competitiveness to maintain high growth in tourist inflow. The estimated relative price level elasticity ranges from 0.2% to 0.8% and is less than one for Denmark and the US. These suggest that a 1% increase in the relative price results in a 0.2% and 0.1% decrease in tourist arrivals to SW6 from Denmark and the US, respectively. The low exchange rate elasticity for Japan, UK and the US may also be a reflection of the depreciation of the Swedish krona against the Japanese yen and US dollar. As expected, the estimated elasticities of CPI_{SW} for the UK and Switzerland are positive.

Parameters	Denmark	UK	Switzerland	Japan	US
Constant	1.848 (0.034)	-2.235 (0.093)	643 (0.784)	-1.964 (0.260)	2.337 (0.110)
CPI	-0.511 (0.256)	2.284 (0.001)	2.601 (0.000)	0.820 (0.272)	-0.5252 (0.373)
Ex	0.241 (0.685)	-0.665 (0.048)	-1.395 (0.092)	- 0.463(0.121)	0.118 (0.579)
Rp	0.204 (0.729)	-1.375 (0.019)	-1.615 (0.013)	-0.994 (0.176)	-0.5272 (0.365)
D1					0.098 (0.056)
D2		0.1549 (0.000)			0.122 (0.042)
D3	0.158 (0.002)	0.210 (0.000)			0.161 (0.004)
D4				-0.476 (0.000)	4
D5	-0.135 (0.018)		0.495 (0.000)	-0.161 (0.025)	0.357 (0.000)
D6	0.308 (0.000)	0.473 (0.000)	1.334 (0.000)	0.235 (0.000)	0.487 (0.000)
D7	0.265 (0.000)	0.443 (0.000)	1.334 (0.000)		0.441 (0.000)
D8			0.721 (0.000)		0.419 (0.000)
D9				-0.227 (0.000)	0.220 (0.001)
D10			-0.331 (0.000)	-0.284 (0.000)	0.172 (0.002)
D11			-0.2136 (0.000)		
$Y_{(t-1)}$	0.212 (0.000)	0.0137 (0.789)	0.1768 (0.000)	0.430 (0.000)	0.334 (0.000)
$Y_{(t-2)}$					-0.157 (0.016)
$Y_{(t-3)}$	-0.135 (0.001)				
$Y_{(t-6)}$	-0.116 (0.002)		-0.183 (0.000)		
$Y_{(t-7)}$	0.144 (0.000)				
$Y_{(t-9)}$	-0.127 (0.005)				
$Y_{(t-10)}$			-0.129 (0.002)		
$Y_{(t-11)}$	0.278 (0.000)			0.187 (0.000)	4
$Y_{(t-12)}$	0.363 (0.000)	0.309 (0.000)		0.263 (0.000)	0.269 (0.000)
R^2	0.924	0.793	0.950	0.808	0.850

The non significant results erased from the Table.

Table 3. ISUR estimation results for Norway

In the case of the UK, we find that all dummies are significant, indicating clear seasonality in the demand for tourism. The demand in December is the highest for the year. we also find lags 4 and 12 are statistically significant. Note that the sign of lag 4 is negative while it is larger and positive for lags 11 and 12. For Switzerland, only the summer dummies are large,

positive, and statistically significant, meaning that the Swiss are relatively more interested in summer tourism. The remaining dummies are either insignificant or small in magnitude. The estimated parameters of lags 1 and 12 are positive and significant.
In general, the lags of the dependent variable for the months of January and December are also significant, supporting the hypothesis of a habit-forming or word-of-mouth effect. Some of the monthly dummies as proxies for seasonal effects are also significant, including January, March, May, June, July, September, October, and November. Estimates of the Denmark dummy show a clear seasonal variation in the pattern of Danish tourism demand in Sweden, such that demand in January, February, March, and July is higher than in December, with lower demand in other months.

4.2 Results for Norway

Table 3 provides estimates of the monthly arrivals from Denmark, Japan, and the US to NWT in Norway. The estimated Norwegian CPI (CPI_{Nor}) long- run elasticity ranges from 0.5% to 0.8% and is lower than that for Denmark, Japan, and the US. The estimated CPI_{SW} coefficients suggest that a 1% increase in CPI_{Nor} results in 0.5%, 0.52%, and 0.8% decreases in tourist arrivals to Norway from Denmark, Japan, and the US, respectively. The low CPI_{Nor} elasticity for Japan and the US may be a reflection of the depreciation of the Norwegian krone against the Japanese yen and the US dollar.
The estimated long run elasticities of the relative price variable for Denmark and the US are less than one (0.2% and 0.6%, respectively), indicating that a 1% rise in the relative price (price of tourism in Norway relative to Sweden) causes about a 1% fall in tourist arrivals from Denmark and the US. The estimated long run –run elasticity of the relative price for Japan is closed to unity (99%), which indicates that a 1% rise in the relative price (price of tourism in Norway relative to Sweden) causes around a 1% drop in tourist arrivals from Japan. The estimated long- run elasticity of the relative price variable for the UK and Switzerland are greater than one, indicating that the arrival of tourists in Norway from these countries is elastic with respect to the relative price variable. This implies that Norway must also maintain its international price competitiveness to maintain high growth in tourist inflow. Yet again, the low exchange rate long- run elasticity for Denmark, Japan, and the US can be a reflection of the depreciation of the Norwegian krona against the Danish krona, the Japanese yen, and the US dollar.

5. Summary and remarks

This chapter has applied the ISUR model, a model not used in other studies that have estimated models for tourism to these two neighbouring regions. First, the model was applied to the neighbouring destinations for the period of transition from characteristics of a lower level of integration and of facing competition from other countries, to characteristics of a high level of integration, globalization, exposure to an international competitive market, and high levels of income and welfare.
Second, the model allowed for comparison of the changes in the behaviour of tourism demand in each country over time, not only in terms of the number of visitors, price and exchange rate, but also of relative price elasticities. The estimated results show the model to be consistent with the data, as indicated by both the diagnostic statistic and the model's good forecasting ability. Moreover, the results are consistent with the properties of

homogeneity and symmetry. This accords with the microeconomic foundations of the model and increases the credibility of the elasticity values.
Substitutability and complementarity among destinations are indicated by positive and negative relative price elasticities, respectively. Clear conclusions about the complementarity or substitutability among destinations are not usually obtained in studies using the ISUR model, which have produced few well defined relative price effects. However, the results in this study seem consistent and also coincide with a priori expectations. Hence they are taken as an indication of the relative magnitudes and directions of changes in demand.
The main purpose of this chapter is to estimate the demand for tourism to two neighbouring regions in Sweden and Norway from five different countries: namely, Denmark, the UK, Switzerland, Japan, and the US. Monthly time series data from 1993:01 to 2006:12 is collected from Statistics Sweden for this purpose. For each visiting country, We specify a separate equation with the relevant information included in each equation. We conduct several diagnostic tests in order to specify the five equations for SW:6 in Sweden and NWT in Norway. We then estimate these equations using Zellner's ISUR, which takes into consideration any possible correlation between the equations and hence is more efficient than other single equation estimation methods, such as OLS.
The results also indicates that CPI, some lagged dependent variables, and several monthly dummy variables representing seasonal effects have a significant impact on the number of visitors to SW6 in Sweden and NWT in Norway. The results also show that the relative price and exchange rate have a significant effect on international tourism demand for some countries. However, although we could view this conclusion as supporting a theoretical framework that describes tourism demand model variable relationships, our demand system lacks a travel cost variable. Nonetheless, our results could also have important implications for the decision-making process of government tourism agencies in both countries when considering influential factors in their long run planning.

6. Appendix

6.1 Diagnostic tests

6.1.1 The Cusum test

This test is used for time series and checks for structural changes. In the Cusum test Recursive Residuals (RR) calculated by the Kalman Filter are used.
I now describe the construction of recursive residuals and the Kalman filter technique. The recursive residuals can be computed by forward or backward recursion. Only forward recursion is described, backward recursion being analogous.
Given N observations, consider the linear model (2 . 2 . 1) but with the corresponding vector of coefficient β expressed as β_t, implying that the coefficients may vary over time t. The hypothesis to be tested is $\beta_1 = \beta_2 = , \ldots , = \beta_N = \beta$. The OLS estimator based on N observations is:

$$b = (X'X)^{-1} X'y,$$

where X is a N by k matrix of observations on the regressors, and y is an N by 1 vector of observations for the dependent variable. Suppose that only r observations are used to estimate β. Then for $r > k$, where k is the number of independent variables,

$$b_r = (X_r'X_r)^{-1} X_r'y_r,$$

$$r = k+1, \ldots, N.$$

Using b_r, one may "forecast" y_r at sample point r, corresponding to the vector X_r of the explanatory variables at that point.
Recursive residuals are now derived by estimating equation (2 . 2 . 1) recursively in the same manner, that is by using the first k observations to get an initial estimate of β, and then gradually enlarging the sample, adding one observation at a time and re-estimating β at each step. In this way, it is possible to get (N-k) estimates of the vector β, and correspondingly (N-k-1) forecast errors of the type:

$$Wr = y_r - X_r b_{r-1}$$

$$r = k+1, \ldots, N$$

where b_{r-1} is an estimate of β based on the first r - 1 observations. It can be shown that, under the null hypothesis, these forecast errors have mean zero and variance $\sigma^2 d_r^2$, where d_r is a scalar function of the explanatory variables, equal to $[1 + X_r'(X'_{r-1}X_{r-1})^{-1} X_r]^{1/2}$.
Then the quantity:

$$W_r = \frac{y_r - X_r b_{r-1}}{[1 + X_r'(X_{r-1}'X_{r-1)})X_r]^{1/2}}$$

$$r = k+1, \ldots, N$$

gives a set of standardized prediction errors, called "recursive residuals". The recursive residuals are independently and normally distributed with mean zero and constant variance σ^2. As a result of a change in the structure over time, these recursive residuals will no longer have zero mean, and the CUSUM of these residuals can be used to test for structural change. CUSUM involves the plot of the quantity:

$$V_r = \sum_{t=k+1}^{r} W_t / \sigma^*$$

$$r = k+1, \ldots, N,$$

where σ^* is the estimated standard deviation based on the full sample.
The test finds parameter instability if the cumulative sum goes outside the area between the two error bounds. Thus, movements of V_t outside the error bounds are a sign of parameter instability.

6.1.2 The Breusch-Godfrey-test

The Breusch-Godfrey test can be separated into several stages:

1. Run an OLS on:

$$y_t = \alpha + \beta X_t + \theta_i y_{t-i} + \varepsilon_t$$

This gives us $\hat{\varepsilon}_t$

2. Run an OLS on:

$$\hat{\varepsilon}_t = \alpha + \beta X_t + \theta_i y_{t-i} + \rho_1 \hat{\varepsilon}_{t-1} + \rho_2 \hat{\varepsilon}_{t-2} + \ldots + \rho_P \hat{\varepsilon}_{t-P} + u_t$$

This equation can be used for any AR(P) process. From this equation the unrestricted residual sum of squares (RSS_u).
The restricted residual sum of squares (RSS_R) is given from the following equation:

$$\hat{\varepsilon}_t = \alpha + \beta X_t + \theta y_{t-1} + v_t$$

The null hypothesis is:

$$H_0 : \rho_1 = \rho_2 = \ldots. = \rho_P = 0$$

3. Run an F-test:

$$F=((RSS_R-RSS_U)/p) \; / \; (RSS_U/(T-k-P))$$

This has a distribution: F(P,T-k-P) under the null hypothesis.
The Breusch-Godfrey test can be tested for AR(P) processes which gives this test a clear advantage over other available tests for autocorrelation.

6.1.3 The Ramsey RESET-test

RESET test stands for Regression Specification Error Test. The test is very general and can only tell you if you have a problem or not. It tests for omitted variables and incorrect functional forms or misspecified dynamics and also if there is a correlation between the error term and the independent variable. The null hypothesis is:

$$H_0: E(\varepsilon_i/X_i) = 0$$

$$H_1: E(\varepsilon_i/X_i) \neq 0$$

(and an omitted variable effect is present)
Thus, by rejecting the null hypothesis indicates some type of misspecification. First a linear regression is specified:

$$y_i = \alpha + \beta X_i + \varepsilon_i$$

This gives the restricted residual sum of squares (RSSR). After the RSS_R has been found the unrestricted model is presented by adding variables (three fitted values):

$$y_t = \alpha + \beta X_i + \theta_1 \hat{y}_i^2 + \theta_2 \hat{y}_i^3 + u_t$$

This gives us the unrestricted residual sum of squares (RSS_U). In the third step the RESET-test uses a F-test:
F= ((RSS_R - RSS_U)/number of restrictions under H_0) / (RSS_U / (N- number of parameters in unrestricted model))
The F-test checks if θ_1=θ_2 =0, if θ_1=θ_2≠0 I have an omitted variable or a misspecification in the model.

6.1.4 The White's test

This test is a general test where I do not need to make any specific assumptions regarding the nature of the heteroscedasticity, whether it is increasing, decreasing etc. The test only tells us if I have an indication of heteroscedasticity.

$$H_0 : \sigma_i^2 = \sigma^2 \quad \forall i$$

The alternative hypothesis is not H_0, anything other than H_0.
The test can be divided into several steps:

1. Run an OLS on:

$$y_i = \alpha + \beta_1 X_{1i} + ... + \beta_k X_{ki} + \varepsilon_i$$

From this equation I get $\hat{\varepsilon}_i$ which is used as a proxy for the variance.

2. Run an OLS on:

$$\hat{\varepsilon}_i^2 = \alpha_0 + \alpha_1 X_{1i} + ... + \alpha_k X_{ki} + \alpha_{k+1} X_{1i}^2 + ... + \alpha_{k+k} X_{k+k}^2 + \alpha_{k+k+1} X_{1i} X_k + \delta_i$$

Where k is the number of parameters. The variance is considered to be a linear function of a number of independent variables, their quadratic and cross products. Thus, the X:s is used as a proxy for Z.

3. Calculate an F-test:

Restricted model:

$$\hat{\varepsilon}_i^2 = \alpha_0^{'} + \delta_i^{'}$$

From this test the restricted residual sum of squares (RSS_R) is measured.
The F-test is:

$$F=((RSS_R-RSS_U)/k) \;/\; (RSS_U/(n-k-1))$$

Where

$$H_0 : \alpha_i = 0 \quad \forall i = 1,2...k$$

6.1.5 The ARCH Engel's LM test

This is a test for AutoRegressive Conditional Heteroscedasticity (ARCH). The ARCH process can be modeled as:

$$y_t = \alpha + \beta X_t + \varepsilon_t$$

where the Variance of ε_t conditioned on ε_{t-i} : Var($\varepsilon_t \setminus \varepsilon_{t-i}$) = $\alpha_0 + \alpha_1 \varepsilon_{t-i}^2$

1. Use OLS on the original model and get: $\hat{\varepsilon}_t$. Square it and use it in the folloing unrestricted model:
2. $\hat{\varepsilon}_t^2 = \alpha_0 + \alpha_i \hat{\varepsilon}_{t-i}^2 + \delta_t$
3. Test whether α_i = 0, for any i = 1, 2, . . . By an F-test as before.

6.1.6 Test for non-normality

The test for non-normality is normally done before one test for heteroskedasticity and structural changes.

The test used here for testing for normal distribution is the Jarque-Bera test. The Jarque-Bera test is structured as follows:

$$T\left[1/6\hat{b}_1^2 + 1/24(\hat{b}_2 - 3)^2\right]$$

$$b_1 = \mu_3 / (\mu_2)^{3/2}$$

$$b_2 = \mu_4 / (\mu_2)^2$$

Where T is the total number of observations, b_1 is a measure for skewness and b_2 is a measure for kurtosis. The μ are different moments. The test has a chi-square distribution with two degrees of freedom under the null hypothesis of normal distribution. The two degrees of freedom comes from having one for skewness and one for kurtosis.

7. References

Andersson, K. and Berg, C. (1995), The inflation target in Sweden. In A.G. Haldane (ed.) Targeting inflation. London: Bank of England

Breusch, T. S. (1978): Testing for Autocorrelation in Dynamic Linear Models, *Australian Economic Papers* 17, 334-355.

Breusch, T. S. and Pagan, A. R. (1980): The Lagrange-Multiplier Test and Its Applications to Model Specification in Econometrics, *Review of Economics Studies*, 47, 239-253.

Brown, R. L., Durbin, J., and Evans, J. M. (1975): Techniques for Testing the Constancy ofRegression Relationships over Time, *Journal of the Royal Statistical Society*, 37,149-192.

Godfrey, L. G. (1978): Testing for Higher Order Serial Correlation in Regression EquationsWhen the Regressors Include Lagged Dependent Variables, *Econometrica*, 46,1303-1310.

Godfrey, L. G. (1988): *Misspecification Tests in Econometrics*, Cambridge: Cambridge University Press.

Grouch, G.I, (1992): Effect of income and price on international tourism to Australia,Tourism Management, June, 196-208.

Gunadhi, H. and Boey, C. (1986) Demand elasticities of tourism in Singapore, Tourism Management, 7, 239 -53

Jarque, C. M., and Bera, A. K. (1987): A Test for Normality of Observations and RegressionResiduals, *International Statistical Review* 55, 163-172.

Kulendran, N. (196) Modelling Quarterly tourist flow to Australia using cointegrationanalysis. TourismEconomic 2 (3), 203-22.Lathiras,P.and Sirioopulos, C. (1998), The demand for a a tourism to Greece: A cointegration approach. Tourism Economics 171-281.

Ramsey, J. B. (1969): Test for Specification error in Classical Linear Least Squares Regression Analysis, *Journal of the Royal Statistical Society (b,* 31, 350-371.

Salman A. Khalik. (2003): Estimating Tourist demand through Cointegration analysis: Swedish Data. Current Issues in Tourism, 6, No. 4.

Salman, A. Shukur G. and Bergmann-Winberg M. (2007): Comparison of Econometric Modelling of demand for domestic and international tourism: Swedish Data. Current Issues in Tourism , 10, No. 4.

Salman, A. Arensson, L. Sörrenson, A and Shukur, G. (2010): Estimating international tourism demand for closer regions in Sweden and Norway with Iterative Seemingly Unrelated Regressions (ISUR). Scandinavian Journal of Hospitality and Tourism, 4 No.10.

Shukur, Ghazi (*2002*): Dynamic Specification and Misspecification in Systems of Demand Equations; A Testing Strategy for Model Selection". *Applied Economics*, 34, 709-725.

Srivastava, V., and Giles, D. (1987). "*Seemingly Unrelated Regression Equations Models*", New York: Marcel Dekker.

Syriopoulos, T(1995): A dynamic model of demand for Mediterranean tourism, international Review of applied economics, 9, 318-36.

Uysal, M. and Crompton,J (1984): determinants of deman for international tourism flows to Turkey, Tourism Management,5 , 288-97

White, H. (1980): A Hetroskedasticity-Consistent Covariance Matrix Estimatore and a Direct Test for Heteroskedastisity, *Econometrica*, 48, 817-838.

Witt, S.F. and Martin, C. A. (1987): Deriving a relative price index for inclusion in international tourism demand estimation models: comment. *Journal of travel research*, 25, No. 3, 38-40.